THE ELEMENTS OF VISUALISATION

Ursula Markham has applied visualisation techniques with significant success in many different situations, including work with sports teams and cancer groups. She also conducts regular stress management workshops for large organisations and is a practising hypnotherapist dealing with every aspect of stress control in men, women and children.

THE ELEMENTS OF

VISUALISATION

Ursula Markham

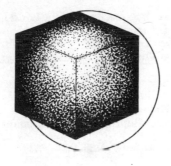

ELEMENT BOOKS

© Ursula Markham 1989

First published in 1989 by
Element Books Limited
Longmead, Shaftesbury, Dorset

Printed and bound in Great Britain by
Billings, Hylton Road, Worcester

Typeset by Selectmove Ltd, London
Designed by Jenny Liddle
Cover design by Max Fairbrother
Cover illustration by Martin Rieser

British Library Cataloguing in Publication Data
Markham, Ursula
The elements of visualisation.
1. Self-development. Use in visualisation
I. Title
158'.1

ISBN 1-85230–076–0

There is only one corner of the Universe you can be certain of improving; and that is your own self.

Aldous Huxley

To the memory of
Steven Lawrence,
a very special friend

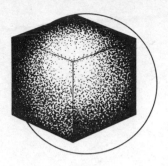

CONTENTS

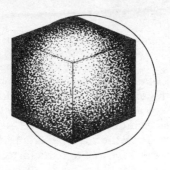

1 · The Main Feature

The lights dim. The curtains which mask the huge screen draw open. You sit in silent anticipation, waiting for the film to begin . . .

But this is a film with a difference. In this production you are the screen-writer, the director and the star. You will decide the twists and turns of the plot; you will create the words and the actions and you will speak those words and perform those actions. And if at any point you are less than satisfied with the way the story is progressing, because you are the one with total control, you have the ability to change the whole course of events. You, therefore, will be responsible for the final effect of this film – whether it leaves you sad or happy, anxious or content.

What is this amazing film and who will give you this wonderful opportunity? The film is the story of your life and the opportunity arises because you are far more in control of the course of your life than you may previously have thought. You can harness the power of your own mind in order to create your chosen scenario and to ensure a satisfactory outcome to most, if not all, of the situations which arise.

Let me give you an example of someone who did just what I have been talking about and, by rewriting the script, managed to change the course of her life and to change it very much for the better.

Cathy had been shy all her life. The only child of doting and over-protective parents, she had been brought up to be quiet and well behaved. She was pretty and intelligent but had never really had many friends. Her mother, a quietly elegant woman who had been nearly forty when Cathy was born, did not relish the idea of a house filled with noisy children, so the child had grown up more accustomed to the company of adults than to others of her own age.

As she grew from a child into a teenager, Cathy found that she was unable to join in the fun which seemed to surround her and in which all her contemporaries appeared to participate. She did not realise at that time that this was due to her upbringing; she felt that there must be something wrong with her – that she was 'different' in some way – and this feeling merely made her retreat more and more into her shell, seeking the company of her parents and their friends instead of making a life for herself.

Cathy grew into a pleasant if somewhat reserved young woman. She got a job in a large company and, although the other girls in the office tried to encourage her to join in the various social gatherings which occur in such companies, the very thought of mixing with all those people she hardly knew filled her with complete and utter horror. She far preferred to stay at home quietly reading or helping her mother in the garden. And yet she was not happy. She was conscious that there was 'something missing' in her life. Although the thinking part of her could not bear to contemplate mixing socially with others, the inner, sensitive part was aware that she was desperately lonely, that she longed to have friends and to be able to talk easily and freely with other people. It seemed to Cathy that everyone else in the world could do this simple thing and that she was isolated in her solitariness.

Eventually Cathy came to see me at my clinic and asked for my help. The fact that she had been able to put her inner feelings into words was an indication that she was reaching a time in her life when she was ready to do something about the situation. So often lonely people will not admit even to themselves, let alone to others, how they feel and until one is able to identify a situation one can do nothing to improve it.

I spent some little time teaching Cathy the visualisation techniques which you will find a little further on in this book. She was an intelligent young woman and an eager and willing pupil. Then I asked her to tell me something she would like to be able to do but which as yet she felt was beyond her. I asked her to start with something comparatively small as there would have been no point in her trying to imagine walking into a room with a hundred people in it – this would have been far too daunting.

Cathy said that there was a young woman in the office who was also quite quiet but who always smiled at her and often tried to engage her in conversation. She felt that she and this other woman, whose name was Donna, would get on quite well and many times she had wished that she could talk to her or ask her to join her for a coffee but, being frightened of a rebuff, she had never plucked up the courage.

I asked Cathy whether she felt she could visualise a scene where she approached Donna in the office and suggested that they did in fact go for a coffee together at the end of the working day. She told me she was prepared to try although she was a little apprehensive about whether or not Donna would agree. Reminding her that she was the script-writer for this particular scene and that she was in control of the plot, I asked Cathy to try and imagine the whole conversation from start to finish – making sure that there was a successful outcome. I suggested that she did it for several days before actually approaching Donna, as I wanted her to be comfortable with the image in her own mind in order that she would feel confident and self-assured when she came to act out the scene.

The next time I saw Cathy she told me that she had in fact spoken to Donna and the two young women had been out together on two separate occasions. They found that they had a great deal in common and they had arranged to go together to the local theatre to see a production of a new play.

This friendship was to be the opening of a door to a whole new world to Cathy. Once she discovered that she did have the ability to approach another person – and once she realised that she was not going to be rejected Cathy went on gradually to enlarge her circle of friends. She would probably never be the type to be the life and soul of some large party but that was not what she had been seeking. She had needed to put an end to the emotionally crippling loneliness which had engulfed her for so many years and to prove to herself that she was capable of giving and receiving friendship.

Just have a look at what Cathy did. She used the greatest tool she possessed – her own imagination – to visualise the situation as she wanted it to be. To return to the analogy of the film production, she wrote the script, directed the action and played the leading role in the production she created. And by doing this – by visualising the positive outcome of the given situation – she was able to bring it about. She had done just what all actors have to do; she had rehearsed and rehearsed her part until she was word perfect. Only in her case she had done it in her mind rather than in reality.

What did all this rehearsal achieve? Why should it be that practising a scene or an event in your mind makes you achieve the result you desire?

Just like Cathy, we have all been 'programmed' all our lives. Sometimes the fears and self-doubts we have will have been created by situations and sometimes by other people. This does not mean that we have necessarily been treated badly by people or that anyone has deliberately set out to hurt us. Cathy's parents loved her dearly but because of the way in which they had brought her up – believing that they were giving her the best of everything and protecting her from the rougher and less elegant side of life – they had in fact created a very great problem for their daughter. Then, of course, that problem grew and grew. Cathy was so unused to mixing with others of her own age that she did not know how to approach them and therefore did so awkwardly. Because of her diffidence and her manner, others would not respond to her with any real warmth or affection. This in turn increased her sense of being 'different', of being the type of person no one wanted to know, making it even more difficult for her to pluck up the courage to approach people in the future.

Although at that time Cathy was probably not consciously visualising scenes in her mind, in effect that is just what she was doing. Every time she thought about approaching someone, perhaps merely to open a conversation with them, on some subconscious level she was prepared to fail, to be rejected as she always had been. And of course this new rejection would merely serve to increase her own poor opinion of herself and what other people must feel about her. By teaching Cathy how to visualise a positive outcome this negative vicious circle was reversed and she was able to envisage a situation in which she would try to open a conversation with another person and the old expected rejection would not take place.

I am not trying to pretend that in Cathy's case we achieved any overnight miracles. The problem had arisen over a long period and it was not going to be dealt with overnight. And it is to Cathy's credit that she persevered with the visualising I asked her to do until she was ready to approach the situation in reality. It is no simple matter to turn a negative attitude into a positive one, but it can be done – and you can do it as well as anyone else.

You too can use visualisation to change your life in many different ways. During the course of this book you will learn how to improve your health, your self-knowledge, your confidence, your relationships – and much, much more. First of all, however, you need to find out all about your wonderful imagination, how it works and how best you can use it.

WHAT IS IMAGINATION?

Your imagination is something you are born with – and of course imagination is not just visual. Although in this book we are dealing mostly with visual and emotional imagination, it does in fact cover all the different senses. Look at the list below and see what your imagination conjures up for you:

Grass being cut: you may imagine the sound of a lawnmower but you are even more likely to imagine the *scent* of the freshly mown grass.

Fresh-baked bread: perhaps you can see in your mind's eye a lovely golden-brown loaf fresh from the oven. But, if you have ever baked bread yourself or been in the house when a new loaf was taken from the oven, I am quite sure that it is the *smell* of the bread which is the thing you recall.

Church bells ringing: in this case you are using the auditory part of your imagination and *hearing* the pealing of the bells.

A baby crying: you may well see a little red screwed-up face but it is the *sound* which will play the most important role in this image.

Chocolate mousse or vinegar: perhaps you will think about how these items look but I am fairly certain that it is the texture and the *taste* which will come to mind. Try this little experiment. Say the word 'vinegar' to someone and watch the expression on their face. Even if it is someone who actually likes the taste of vinegar, they will grimace as though they could actually sense the acidity.

Lying on a sunny beach: naturally the picture is likely to come into your mind of a glorious summer's day on a sandy beach, but you will also be able to imagine *feeling* the heat on your body as you lie there.

Walking through a snowstorm: in addition to the visual image you will have a *sense of the cold and chill* of the situation and it is the latter which is likely to dominate.

A happy or sad situation you have actually experienced: In this case it is the *emotion* which will play the strongest part in the imagined

5

scene. Indeed the child actress Margaret O'Brien, who was renowned for her ability to be able to cry on request, claimed that her talent was due to the fact that she was able to remember some sad incident and this would make her cry all over again.

All the senses play an important role in imagination, but in this book we are going to deal mostly with the visual and the emotional aspects of imagination, as these are the ones which are most likely to help you achieve your aims.

There are many people who claim that they have not got a good visual imagination – that they are unable to 'see pictures' in their mind. And yet it is a proven fact that the only people who are unable to see images clearly in their mind are those who had the misfortune to be born blind. Even those who lost their sight at a comparatively early age have the ability to create visual images in their imagination. The trouble is that so many people lose that ability through lack of practice. After all, any athlete or gymnast who does not continue to exercise his or her muscles regularly will find that those muscles become weaker and he will be less able to perform as he previously did. Ask anyone who has had the misfortune to spend a considerable amount of time in a hospital bed how their legs felt when at last they were allowed to get up and walk around. You will find that in the majority of cases the muscles of the legs had become so weak that the person was hardly able to stand, let alone walk.

Your imagination is just like the muscles of your body. If you do not make full and regular use of it, it will become weak and flabby and then, when you do want to use it to help you, you will have great difficulty in doing so. But, just like any other muscle in the body, your visual imagination can be greatly strengthened, first of all by specific exercises and later by regular use. Later, in Chapter 3, you will find a series of simple exercises, each of which will only take minutes of your time but which, when practised regularly, will enable you to reawaken and make full use of that most precious of possessions – your visual imagination.

There exist two types of people who are most generally credited with having a fertile and vivid imagination – artists and children.

Any artist, whether it be a writer, painter, sculptor, poet or any other person with a highly developed sense of creativity, must use his imagination in order to be creative. Any picture ever painted was first imagined; any piece of music ever composed was first heard in the mind of the composer; any statue sculpted from a piece of hard, cold stone was first of all visualised by the sculptor concerned. All those people, and all creators and designers of every type, have a highly developed visual imagination and they keep it that way and even improve upon it by frequent and regular use.

And what of the children? Show any small child a picture and ask him to make up a story about it and you will immediately realise what a fertile imagination that child has. Unfortunately, because of the era of competitiveness and formal education in which we live, that imagination often becomes dulled and dusty through diminution of use at a very early age. 'Don't daydream'; 'Concentrate on what you are doing'; 'Use your common sense'. These are the words repeated over and over again to our children as they sit in their classrooms. Of course, I do not mean to suggest in any way that we should not learn to use our sense of logic or to be able to compete with others where necessary. But how much better it would be if all schools could do as some enlightened ones are in fact doing and encourage the children to preserve their ability to imagine, to visualise and to develop their sense of creativity.

A child knows how to imagine before he knows how to reason. He is born with a naturally vivid and fertile imagination but he has to learn how to use logic and reason. And, while both imagination and reason have important roles to play in our lives, so often the education and development of the latter means that the former is lost altogether. And the older we get and the more we compete the more this is so.

Your brain is divided into two separate sections – the left and the right. And these two sections of your brain govern completely different aspects of you and your way of thinking. The lists below, based upon the work of Robert E. Ornstein in his book *The Psychology of Consciousness*, will show you the different ways in which we use each side of the brain.

The Left Brain

Connected to the right side of the body and the right side of each eye's vision.

Deals with inputs one at a time.

Processes information in a linear manner. Has a linear and sequential mode of operation.

Deals with time. Responsible for the faculty of verbal expression, or language.

Responsible for verbal and mathematical functions.

Specialises in memory and recognition of words or numbers.

Normally tends to specialise in logic and analytical reasoning or thinking.

The seat of reason.

The crucial side of the brain for wordsmiths, mathematicians, and scientists.

THE RIGHT BRAIN

Connected to the left side of the body and the left side of each eye's vision.

Enables ready integration of many inputs at once.

Processes information more diffusely. Has a non-linear and simultaneous mode of operation.

Deals with space. Responsible for gestures, facial and body movements (or 'body language'), tone of voice, etc.

Responsible for spatial and relational functions; awareness of our bodies; for sports and dancing; our orientation in space; recognition of faces; artistic endeavour; musical ability and recognition of pitch.

Specialises in memory and recognition of objects, persons and places, music, etc.

Normally tends to specialise in intuition and holistic perception or thinking.

The seat of passion and of dreams.

The crucial side of the brain for artists, crafts people, musicians.

This explanation can be simplified into the diagram overleaf, which will show you even more clearly which side of the brain we are taught to use predominantly in our twentieth-century lives.

As you will see from reading the list, it is the right-hand side of our brains which suffers from lack of use as we are taught to concentrate more and more on the functions of the left. Yet it is the right-hand side of the brain and its correct use and implementation which will enable you to change your life and the way in which you cope with any problems you may have.

LEFT	RIGHT
Logic	Emotions
Analysis	Creativity
Reason	Sense of rhythm
Academic learning	Imagination
Language	Intuition
Calculation	Dreaming
Memory	Sensitivity

By concentrating on left-brain use we are only fulfilling half our potential. Imagine how unbalanced your body would be if you had developed the muscles on one side only – you would limp and you would have strength in only one arm. By using one side of our brain only – whichever one that may be – we are unbalancing ourselves mentally and emotionally. But the other side of our brain is always there, just waiting to be rediscovered and to be allowed to function fully, and once this has happened we are able to rediscover the full potential of our minds. Many famous and creative people have extolled the virtues of doing more than just thinking; from Tchaikovsky to Jung, Einstein to Mozart, they have claimed that their most inspired moments came at times when they were not thinking consciously about their work at all.

Of course, visualisation can be negative as well as positive and many people do themselves untold harm by allowing this negative visualisation to become part of their lives. Think about the person who says 'I'm so clumsy, I always drop things', or the one who claims 'I always let myself down at interviews' – both these are examples of negative visualisation. These people have programmed themselves over the years to become failures. The one who has decided that he is clumsy will become so tense and anxious when carrying some precious item that he is in fact far more likely to drop it. The person who is convinced that he or she always does badly at interviews will anticipate failure before the event and will therefore not present himself well and, when he is rejected yet again, this will only serve to add to his already low opinion of himself.

There is an old music-hall song, made famous by Stanley Holloway, called 'My word, you do look queer'. It tells of a man who sets out one day, feeling well and positive, and each person he meets tells him how ill he is looking. Gradually, as the day goes on, he begins to feel less and less well as the words of all these other people start to penetrate his consciousness. It is only when he runs into a friend who tells him that he is looking fit and well that his original sense of well-being returns and he is his old healthy and jolly self again.

That song, which was intended to be humorous, contains far more truth than is often thought. We are all influenced by the thoughts and opinions of others as well as of ourselves. Think of the children whose impatient parents or teachers may have said to them 'You'll never be any good at mathematics (or chemistry, or geography)' or – worse still – 'You're stupid'.

Gina was thirty-two years old when I met her. Coming from a family who set great store by education, she had been encouraged as a child and had done well at school as well as developing a considerable musical talent. She had married at twenty-one a man ten years her senior. Her husband, an academic and somewhat chauvinistic man with a low degree of tolerance for anyone whom he considered less intellectual than himself, had spent many years telling Gina that she was stupid. Now, although she did not consider herself to be brilliant academically, Gina knew perfectly well that she was not stupid. Yet by the time I first encountered her when she came to my clinic she had lost all confidence in herself and her abilities. Once she realised what had been happening, however, and how greatly her own self-image had been affected by those constantly repeated accusations of stupidity, it took very little time for her to be able to revise her own opinions of herself and to look positively towards the future once more.

It is amazing how many people are brought up not to expect happiness and even to feel guilty if they do feel happy. So much so that, should the faintest glimmerings of anything more than the merest satisfaction with their lot in life start to appear, they will actually set about making sure that they do not become happy. We have all met such people who seem bent upon their own self-destruction; the woman who enters relationship after relationship with the most unsuitable men, knowing that it will end in disaster, and indeed almost willing it to do so, as this will serve to reinforce her own view of herself that she is unlovable and unworthy of happiness within a caring relationship. Or the man who has one extramarital affair after another, knowing only too well that when he is found out (while in many cases making sure that he will be) it will mean the beginning of the end of his marriage. Both these people have grown up to be so afraid of happiness and so convinced that they do not deserve it that they ensure that it is not theirs for too long.

We all have to take responsibility for our own lives and to be willing to change. Even if you feel that others were to blame for your own negative attitude, you have to be convinced that you want to change, that you have the ability to change and that you are prepared to work to bring about that change.

If this ability to alter the course of our lives by positive visualisation has been around for such a long time, why is it that until recently it has been largely ignored by all but a few? The reason is that we have all become so obsessed with logic, calculation and the thinking process that we have given little time in our daily life to imagination. And yet so much of that thinking process is concerned with thoughts which are trivial and unimportant. Try this simple test for yourself:

Close your eyes and try to make your mind blank. Imagine nothing but colour – whatever colour you choose. Unless you have been practising a high degree of meditation for some considerable time, you will find that it is just not possible to make your mind a blank and that many thoughts will intrude. Don't try to avoid this; just let them in, note them and let them go again.

You may be surprised when you try this exercise at just how trivial are the thoughts which enter your mind. They are unlikely to be the world-changing, decision-making, wonderfully enlightened examples of the logical thinking process. They are far more likely to concern mundane and relatively unimportant things. How much more usefully that time could have been spent visualising you and your life as you would like it to be, or even just generally daydreaming about nothing in particular.

Who can best make use of this ability to visualise? The answer is simple – YOU! I have met the executive of a large business concern who uses visualisation constantly for both himself and his employees in order to expand his company. I have worked with sportsmen of all types who have proved to themselves beyond any conceivable doubt that, although naturally visualisation can never replace training and skill, what it can do is to ensure that each person, whatever his sport, can perform to the best of his own ability and often far better than he had ever previously thought possible. I know a woman who lost over four stone, using visualisation to help her stick to a sensible eating programme without any of the feelings of deprivation which normally accompany a diet. I have worked personally with sufferers from cancer, multiple sclerosis and leukaemia – as well as from illnesses of many other types – who have experienced excellent remissions and improvements in their health by taking responsibility for the way in which the disease was likely to affect them and by using their imagination to bring about an improvement in many cases – and a complete cure in some.

So, whatever your problem and however you think it may have been caused, now is the time for you to use your own imagination to bring about the changes which until now you may have considered impossible. Take responsibility for your own future, write your screenplay, sit in the director's chair, put on your greasepaint – it is time to begin!

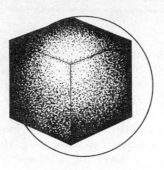

2 · Sleep on It – The Value of Dreams

Everyone can dream. Indeed, everyone does dream. Those who insist that they never dream at all actually dream just as frequently as the rest of us, although they may not remember anything about it. Even those of us who are quite aware of dreaming night after night very seldom remember those dreams in any real detail but merely retain a vague jumble of seemingly unrelated impressions. Dreams are not merely visual – we dream with all our senses, so that we are aware of sound, touch, smell, and taste. Those who were born blind simply dream with four senses instead of five.

One of the world's oldest known written documents is the *Egyptian Book of Dreams*. This volume is about five thousand years old, so you can see that dreams were known to have a special significance even then. Many ancient civilisations believed that one should never wake a sleeping person as, during sleep, the soul has left the body and is elsewhere and might not be able to return in time should the sleeper be suddenly awoken. Even today, many spiritualists believe that the spirit is able to travel in the sleep state and that it does so in order to develop greater knowledge and to enhance its evolution.

13

This chapter is not about dream interpretation. From the time when Joseph explained to Pharaoh the meaning of his dreams, to the present day, people have been trying to interpret dreams and to explain their significance. There are many books available on the subject of dream interpretation, although unfortunately there are almost as many meanings attributed to a particular dream as there are books. What we are discussing here, however, is the value of dreams in solving your problems, answering your questions and reshaping your life. A little further on I shall be giving you some simple methods of directing the path of your dreams and remembering them when you wake so that you are more able to benefit from them.

What is a dream? The dictionary describes it as 'a train of thoughts and fancies during sleep, a vision: a distant hope or ideal; to contemplate as imaginably possible'. In fact, it is something remarkably similar to visualisation, with the one major difference that dreams take place in the subconscious mind whereas visualisation is definitely conscious. Just think how many hours of the twenty-four you spend asleep; if you could only harness and make use of that sleeping time, how much more likely you would be to achieve your aims. (Remember that we are talking here about natural sleep rather than that which is induced by certain drugs such as sleeping pills or antidepressants.)

Like visualisation, dreams are governed by the right-hand side of the brain. As you have already seen, it is this side which develops creativity in the individual. You want to create a better life for yourself so you must learn to make your dreams work for you.

You may wonder why it is that, if dreams are so significant and can be so helpful, they always appear to be so jumbled in your mind when you wake. Because, without practice, you do not have total recall of that which you have been dreaming, you have been trying to explain logically something which is only half remembered. In fact, developing total recall of your dreams is something which can be learned, as you will find if you follow the simple exercises at the end of this chapter.

Dreams are self-centred. If the dreamer is not the central character in the 'plot', then the entire dream will revolve around how the events affect him and what his reactions are. And the dreamer can – and often does – experience every emotion; he can feel love, fear, anger, or hate. Because those half-remembered images are often an expression of what is going on (or what you hope or fear is going on) in your life, dreams can be disturbing or distressing. To minimise this, however many problems you have in your life at the time, try practising one of the simple relaxation exercises described at the end of this chapter before you go to sleep. Even if your problems are not immediately resolved, it seems that you will be able to put them further from your mind so that your sleep will be less troubled.

To improve your life in whatever way you choose you need to learn to mimic the dreams of your subconscious with conscious visualisation. In a dream nothing is impossible. In the same way, with visualisation you can convince yourself that nothing is impossible – that you are capable of anything. Because visualisation requires conscious effort on your part, you are in charge of the way in which you 'programme' your mind. Therefore you will not find yourself indulging in the pure flights of fancy of subconscious dreaming but you will be freeing yourself of the negativity which is likely to hold you back in your journey through life.

Think of your mind as a computer. When you have problems, you are only too aware of the questions but you have access to few, if any, of the answers. Feed all the information into your mind, go to sleep and let the computer do its work with no interference from the conscious (left-brain) mind or from self-induced negativity. Remember, too, that dreaming need not only apply to night-time. Your inner computer can function just as well when you catnap or when you doze.

Many famous people have developed ideas and obtained inspiration from their dreams:

Thomas Edison claimed that, if he made a note of those problems which concerned him the most before he went to sleep, when he awoke he would have discovered the answer.

Otto Loewi was awarded the Nobel Peace Prize for his discovery that active chemicals are involved in the actions of nerves. He said that he had been working on this subject for some time without being able to answer all the questions, only to find that everything came together when he learned to harness the power of his mind and to understand his dreams.

Robert Louis Stevenson insisted that most of his plots came to him either in dreams or immediately upon waking. This latter claim only serves to prove the point that it is not always the dreams themselves which are important. It is as though dreaming enables you to enter some sort of subconscious sorting-house, so that the ideas arrived at when you wake are of great significance and clarity.

Freud explained that those wishes and desires which could not be acted upon in ordinary life could be freely expressed in dreams and that this often acted therapeutically for the dreamer, allowing him to release those pent-up emotions which, if repressed, could cause him psychological harm.

Extensive research has been carried out, primarily in the United States and in the Soviet Union. Experiments using willing volunteers have shown that when an individual is prevented from dreaming he is likely to undergo a dramatic personality change, often becoming either violent and aggressive or morose and withdrawn. When you consider that it has been found that the majority of antidepressants decrease the amount of dreaming, it is easy to see why they often have the side effects they do.

If you can only learn to harness and direct your dreams, you can change the pattern of your life. To do this involves three stages:

1. RELAXATION

Learning to relax is a vitally important part of creatively directing your dreams. It is only when you relax that you can ensure that your conscious mind does not interfere with the subconscious process of dreaming. In addition, by making a definite effort to relax prior to sleeping, your are less likely to have unpleasant or disturbing dreams and more likely to find that they are both enjoyable and constructive.

There are many different ways of relaxing and it does not really matter which one you choose. A few are listed below and it is up to you to try each in turn and see which one suits you best. Give each method a real chance by practising it for four to seven nights before progressing to the next. Naturally you should wait until you are in bed and prepared for sleep before using whichever relaxation technique appeals to you.

(a) Lie in your bed with your eyes closed. Make sure that you are warm enough but that the room is not overheated or stuffy. Starting with your feet and working upwards through your body, tense and relax each set of muscles in turn. Take your time and allow yourself to become extremely conscious of the difference in sensations when your muscles are rigid and when they are loose and relaxed. Allow a little extra time for concentrating on the muscles of your neck, shoulders, jaw, and face, as it is in these areas that tension is usually the greatest.

By the time you have worked all the way up your body so that you are as free from tension as possible, you should begin to feel a pleasant warmth permeating those newly relaxed muscles.

(b) Having relaxed your body as above, concentrate on the pattern of your breathing. Let your breathing become slow and rhythmic. It does not matter particularly whether you breathe deeply or not; it is the establishment of a slow, regular rhythm which is important. In fact, the more you relax, the shallower your breathing is likely to become. You may find it helpful to count, silently in your head, 'one' as you breathe in and 'two' as you breathe out, until the gentle, even rhythm is established. Then you can gradually cease counting and let the regularity of your breathing take over.

(c) Once you have relaxed, as indicated in (a) above, use your imagination to help you feel that your body is growing heavier and heavier. Begin once again with your feet, imagining them as heavy as lead weights. Once you have established that this area has begun to feel heavy, then you can progress up your body, little by little, until that feeling of heaviness has spread from your toes to the top of your head.

(d) Choose a cassette of a piece of music which you find particularly soothing and play it quietly as you relax in your bed. Allow your mind to form images as you listen to the music – it does not matter whether these are pictorial images or whether, like many people, you simply become aware of colours and patterns in your mind.

(e) Having relaxed your body as described in (a) above, and with your eyes still closed, imagine that you are looking at a curtain or a piece of cloth which is bright red and gold in colour. As you look at it, be aware that the colours are changing to shades of blue and green. Then let it change again to tones of violet and purple.

This method is perhaps a little more difficult than the others and may well require more perseverance on your part but, if you can manage it, it is an extremely effective aid to relaxation and preparation for sleep.

2. PROGRAMMING YOUR DREAMS

This is not quite as straightforward as it may sound, as you are dealing with your subconscious rather than your conscious mind. Whereas during deliberate visualisation you are completely in control of the images which enter your mind, this is not the case at all when you dream. So do not be concerned if the dreams you have appear to have no connection whatsoever with your own particular problem. The connection will be there – it may just be that you are unable to recognise it at first glance. While your subconscious is sorting things out, the images may well be of a symbolic rather than a literal nature.

(a) Encouraging a Specific Outcome

Use this method when you are fully aware of the area of your life you wish to improve.

Once your body is totally relaxed, using one of the methods already described, begin to see yourself in your mind in the particular situation which concerns you – but make sure that you imagine the circumstances precisely as you would like them to be, rather than as you fear they might be.

Let us take an example. Suppose you are interested in playing golf but find that your putting is not as accurate as it used to be. In your mind, before you sleep, see yourself playing golf and putting perfectly from any position on the green. It is extremely important that you see a moving rather than a still 'picture'. In other words, that you see the whole thing taking place in your mind, one stage at a time, starting with the stance, mentally sizing up the position, the practice swings and then the shot itself – ending, of course, with the ball rolling nicely into the hole.

I am not suggesting for a moment that any form of visualisation or dream programming will work if you do not have the ability to play golf in the first place. What the process will do is make you perform to the very best of your ability in the future. If you have had lessons in golf, you will not have to calculate each and every move involved in successful putting; your body will do that automatically once you are convinced that you can do it.

This form of dream programming does take practice, so you cannot expect everything to be perfect on the first occasion. Nor will you necessarily see dramatic results on the very next day. But, if you persevere, you will find that two significant things happen. The first is that your dreams will become a continuation of the pre-sleep visualisation, so that your unconscious mind becomes filled with the images of you as a successful golfer. The second is that your actual prowess on the putting green noticeably improves.

Remember that, if you want your dreams to work for you, it is essential that you see the images clearly in your mind. Statements and affirmations will not suffice. There is a belief that repeating a phrase over and over to yourself – in the style of Emil Coué – will achieve the same effect. Theoretically this method would work – if it were not for the fallibility of human beings. For affirmations to be really effective, it is necessary to concentrate upon the meaning and significance of the words as you say them. Unfortunately, as one repeats a word or phrase again and again, it ceases to have any real meaning and the mind detaches itself from what is being said, thus nullifying the possible beneficial effects.

(b) *General Problem-Solving*

This method will not necessarily come up with any definite answers but should help you to find a sense of direction in a specific situation and, used in conjunction with conscious visualisation, to make order out of disorder in a particular area of your life.

Prior to sleep, having relaxed by whichever method you find most suitable, allow your mind to dwell on the aspect of your life which causes you unease. Once again it is important to try and fill your head with images rather than to verbalise the situation.

Let us suppose that you have a particular problem to solve or a decision to make with regard to an important relationship in your life. Consciously you may be considering various solutions, but these will be taking into account all sorts of extraneous influences which should really have no bearing upon the matter at all. All the time, however, your subconscious mind will *know* the best solution for you personally and, indeed, for all concerned, but it is extremely difficult for any individual to clear his mind of the irrelevances which clutter it up.

When you begin to programme your dream, do not attempt to 'design' the ideal solution to your problem. It is far better to concentrate on the situation as it is now and let your subconscious take care of the future. It is just like keying all the known facts into a vast computer and letting the answers present themselves to you on the screen.

It is quite likely that your dreams in this instance will not appear to concern themselves with the problem which is uppermost in your mind. They are far more likely to involve people and events from your past – but this is all part of arriving at a conclusion. After all, the emotional 'you' which exists today is a product of those earlier people and events, and so your mental computer is doing its work, even if it appears to use a roundabout method.

Once again, it is important to allow your subconscious mind sufficient time to find the most appropriate outcome to your problem. It could take as little as a day or two – or it could even be a matter of weeks before you are certain in your own mind as to the best way of dealing with the situation. But, provided you use your dreamtime in the way I have indicated, you can be sure that your highly efficient internal computer will not let you down. The day will dawn when you will *know* what direction you have to take – even if you cannot be absolutely certain how you know it. It is then up to you as an individual to act upon that knowledge.

3. REMEMBERING YOUR DREAMS

Most people, when they wake, are aware that they have been dreaming, but few, if any, remember their dreams in any great detail. And yet, what great benefit we might all derive from a more intimate acquaintance with the workings of our subconscious.

Remembering your dreams takes practice and preparation. It seems that the very act of getting out of bed and beginning the practical part of your day is sufficient to destroy the already nebulous images hiding in the depths of your mind. So you must be in a position where you have the time and the facility to concentrate on what you can recall of your dream and to make a note of it.

Before you go to sleep at night, get into the habit of placing a pen and notebook by the side of the bed – right beside the alarm clock, if necessary. Or, if you prefer it, you can use a small cassette recorder; some people find that they are happier to talk about their dreams than to write about them. Try both methods and see which comes more naturally to you.

You are going to need a few moments in which to think about the dream you have had and then to make your notes, whether written or verbal, so you may well have to set your alarm clock to wake you a little earlier – ten minutes at the most should be sufficient.

Try to get into the habit of waking up and then lying in bed with your eyes closed, concentrating on the last remembered image of your dream. Consciously make an effort to fix that image in your mind before sitting up and making a note of it. It may be that, in the early stages, that single image is all you can recall – but don't be downhearted. You will eventually find that an isolated image will lead you to remember other scenes or emotions contained in your dream and you can then make a note of these too.

It is important, when you first begin to practise this technique, that you do not concern yourself too much with trying to interpret your dreams or understand their significance. Be content merely to make notes. As time goes by, you will find that you are able to remember more and more and that meanings will become increasingly apparent to you.

Some people like to keep a 'dream diary' and to get into a routine of recording their dreams every morning before rising. This can often be beneficial as, even at times when there are no outstanding problems to deal with, your subconscious will always be working on your behalf. Looking back at a series of dreams at the end of a period of time could well give you a clear indication of ways in which you could improve the quality of your life.

Dreams are by no means the vague and transient things that many people have long believed them to be. By learning how to programme and remember them you could well be harnessing one of the most beneficial aspects of your subconscious mind, and this, coupled with the technique of visualisation, could enable you to change your life in many ways.

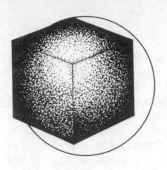

3 • REDISCOVER YOUR IMAGINATION

If you are the director of this wonderful film in which you also have the starring role, you will not be too happy with the results if the whole thing is shot through a camera with a dirty lens! Similarly, if you are to learn to harness the enormous powers of your own imagination, the outcome will be much more satisfactory if you have sharpened your ability to visualise before you begin. The clearer the image you are able to create in your mind, the greater and more effective will be the benefits of the visualisation process itself.

What is your opinion of your own ability to visualise clearly? Some people are quite happy about their ability, whereas others will insist that they are just not able to 'see' anything at all in their imagination. In this chapter you will find a series of simple exercises designed to enable the latter group of people to improve their visual imagination to an extent that they would never have considered possible. It will also helped the former group to improve the clarity and intensity of the images they are able to create. After all, there is no point in my telling you all about the benefits of visualisation if you do not feel that you are able to visualise properly in the first place.

Remember that the only people who can never see pictorial images in their minds are those who were born blind. Even those who have lost their sight at quite an early age are able to create pictures in their imagination, although, in fact, what they imagine may differ somewhat from reality. Everyone else, without exception, has the innate ability to visualise. Of course, many people may have lost that ability over the years, particularly if they were brought up not to 'daydream' and to be practical rather than imaginative or creative. But that ability can be regained. Just think of it as a muscle which, through lack of constant use, has become weak and flabby. With regular exercise and practice, that muscle can become strong and effective again. In just the same way, if you are willing to practise using your visual powers, you can rediscover the precious gift of imagination. But, just like any muscle in the body, the imagination is not going to return to full strength in the course of twenty-four hours. It will need regular exercise over a period of time but, because you will be relearning a forgotten technique rather than tackling something new, you will find the process much easier than you might think. And the results will certainly make the effort well worth while.

All you need to give, in the beginning, is ten minutes of your time twice a day. However hectic and busy your day, I can assure you that the changes you are going to make in your life will make it well worth while getting up ten minutes earlier or going to bed ten minutes later, if necessary. Use that time to work through the following exercises. Please don't be impatient, but wait until one exercise comes easily to you before continuing to the next.

EXERCISE 1

(a) Sit at a desk or table and place a single object on the surface – perhaps a cup or jug. Spend several minutes studying that item. Don't just say to yourself 'Oh, yes; that is a cup.' *Look* at it; *study* it. Pay attention to the shape of that cup, to its texture. Is there a pattern on it? What is the handle like – is it simple or ornate? If the cup is (for example) blue, take note of the particular shade of blue. Is the colour constant, or is it perhaps lighter at the top and deeper at the bottom?

Once you feel that you are really familiar with the particular item you have chosen, close your eyes and try to picture it in your mind. Don't worry if you find difficulty in visualising the object to start with; if you are unable to create the image satisfactorily, simply open your eyes and take another look. Continue with this exercise until you are quite happy with the results before going on to the one which follows.

In the beginning you will be using not just your imagination but also a combination of memory and logic. Eventually, however, you will find that you are able simply to close your eyes and visualise your chosen object without going through the process of remembering what it looks like.

(b) Sit in one of your own rooms. It is quite a good idea to use the bedroom as there is less likely to be interference from radio, television or even other people here, and your exercise will be greatly helped by a feeling of peace and tranquillity. Always sit in the same place in the room, whether it is on a chair or on the bed. Look around you at what you can see. Study the size and the shape of each piece of furniture. Really look at the colours and textures of the materials in the room. It is even a good idea to think about how that room makes you feel; do you feel comfortable there? Is it a haven of peace after the hurly-burly of the day? When you eventually go on to use visualisation to improve your own life, you will need to be able to make a link between images and emotions, so it is helpful to begin to forge that link now.

Once you think that you really know how your chosen room looks and feels, close your eyes and try to picture it in as much detail as possible, visualising not simply its appearance but the texture of its furnishings and the atmosphere created. This exercise is a little more difficult than the previous one and may therefore take more practice on your part, but soon it too will be well within your capabilities.

(c) The third part of this exercise is the most difficult of all, because you are going to deal with something which, although constant in part, contains ever-changing elements too.

Sit by any window in your own home and look at the world outside. Until now you have been practising studying and recreating in your mind objects which have been still and unchanging. Now you have to deal with something which still has a basic sameness to it – the street, the grass, the trees, and the buildings will all remain constant. But, whatever the scene before you, some things will alter – either as you look at them (pedestrians walking, birds flying) or over a period of days (flowers opening, weather changing).

Follow precisely the same routine as you did with parts (a) and (b). Study the view from your window until you know it well and until you can see it clearly in your mind when you close your eyes. Once you have observed changes in the scene itself, try and visualise those changes in your mind too. In other words, if you happen to look out at your garden on a bright sunny day, once you have successfully closed your eyes and visualised the scene as it is, try and picture the same view of your garden, but with the rain falling.

When you reach a stage where you feel confident in your ability to visualise (a), (b), and (c) above, you may go on to the following exercises. These should take you far less time to perfect and you should find them much easier to do than the earlier ones, because you will already have overcome the greatest hurdle and that was to start your visual imagination functioning again.

EXERCISE 2

(a) You will remember that in the first part of the first exercise you had to visualise a specific object – a cup, for example – after having looked at it. Your task this time is to visualise a different cup or jug – but this time to do so *before* looking at it. Close your eyes and see the object clearly in your imagination. Then open your eyes once more and go and find that item and look at it. Were you right? If not, take note of those details which confused you. But don't worry if you could not visualise this item perfectly; the fact that you were able to picture it at all is what matters.

Continue with this exercise (using a different object each time) until you feel that you have achieved a certain measure of success in your ability to visualise a variety of items.

(b) In an earlier exercise you had to sit in a room, study it and then see it in your mind, being aware of the atmosphere as well as the appearance of the room. Now I would like you to sit in one room and then, closing your eyes, visualise a *different* room with which you are familiar. What does it look like? What does it *feel* like? Take your time and remember the enormous variety of textures to be found in any room: the softness of cushions, the roughness of some stone or wooden surfaces, the polished smoothness of others. Think of the way in which some rooms conjure up an atmosphere of brightness and light while others have a darker and more sombre air. Consider all these things before going and looking at the room itself. It is not really important if you were not able to remember every detail of the selected room; what does matter is that you were able to picture it and to capture its atmosphere successfully.

(c) Having already studied the view from one window in your home, it is now time to close your eyes and try to picture what you would see if you were to look out of a different window. Of course, you cannot be certain of those things which are constantly changing, but the basics remain constant. Once you can see those basics in your mind (the street, the houses), try and imagine the changing objects (the people, the blossom on the trees). Above all, what is the feeling generated by that scene? If it is a garden, do you imagine it towards the close of the day, with long purple shadows spreading across the lawn, or on a blustery spring morning with trees swaying and washing flapping on the line? If it is a street, do you visualise it on a Sunday afternoon with people strolling along in a leisurely fashion, or at eight-thirty in the morning when everyone is hurrying, head down, to work?

The next step, having visualised this new and different vista, is to go and look from the chosen window and to see how the view compares with what you have imagined. Once again, it is not the fact of whether or not you are correct in every minute detail which is particularly important, but the fact that you have been able to create the image of the scene at all.

Once you become accustomed to this particular exercise, experiment to see whether in your imagination you can change the time of day or the season of the year. If it is winter and all the passers-by are muffled in thick coats, scarves and hats, imagine the same scene on a sunny afternoon in July when the women are in sleeveless dresses and the children skipping along in shorts and tee-shirts.

EXERCISE 3

(a) You have now been able to create an image in your mind of a single item which is in your possession at the present time. For this part of the exercise I would like you to try and remember an item from your childhood – perhaps an ornament which stood in your family home; perhaps a favourite toy of your own. Try and picture the item and then to visualise its immediate surroundings. Was it something which was permanently on display or was it kept in a drawer or cupboard until needed. What did it look like? What did it feel like? What emotions did it create in you at the time – and how does it make you feel now? All these points are important and, even if you do not have the object now so that actual comparisons are impossible, your own personal image of it and reactions to it will become clearer and stronger each time you practise.

(b) Having practised visualising a room which is part of your present environment, it is time to try and see in your imagination a room in the home you lived in as a child. Perhaps the easiest room to remember will be either your own bedroom or the kitchen. Researchers have proved that the strongest childhood memories seem to involve the areas of play, sleep, and preparation of food. It does not appear to be the actual eating of the food which is significant but the place where it is prepared. And, of course, if you think of toddlers and small children who tend to follow mother around the home, a great deal of their time would be spent in the kitchen.

However, the choice of room is entirely up to you. But try and visualise what it looked like, who was to be found in it, what you did in it, and how you felt about it then. Then ask yourself what feelings those remembered images conjure up for you today.

(c) By practising previous exercises you have become accustomed to visualising a scene and to imagining changes in that scene which are brought about by differences in weather conditions, in the time of year, or the presence of people or animals. Try now to picture a scene from your childhood. It is important to be as spontaneous as possible about this. If I were to say to you 'think of a scene from your childhood' – *that* is the one I want you to choose rather than spending time selecting an appropriate image.

Treat this remembered scene just as you did the observed ones. There will be certain things which will remain constant. Perhaps you are in your own back garden; it could be that you have chosen to remember the walk to school; or perhaps you are looking out of your childhood bedroom window. In all of those scenes, just as in any other, the basic features will remain the same. The sand and the sea, the roads to be crossed, or the houses in your street – they will not change. But the effect upon those fixed objects of sunshine or snow, people or vehicles, will be quite dramatic. It should prove interesting to you to see which type of picture comes most readily to mind.

As with the previous two sections of this particular exercise, concentrate not only upon the visual image you are able to create, but also upon the sensations and the atmosphere created in and around you – both then and now. Try changing the weather conditions or the time of day or year in your chosen image and see whether you feel differently about it.

EXERCISE 4

This exercise is slightly different as there is no way in which you can judge yourself to be 'right' or 'wrong'. But, once you have successfully completed all three parts, you can be sure that your imagination is once again in full working order and that it can therefore be used to great advantage in helping you to create through positive visualisation the type of life you would like to live.

(a) Until now you have had actual objects – current or remembered – to help you in your visualisation. The next stage is to create a single object, whether practical or ornamental, in your imagination. For the sake of simplicity, let us keep to the image of a cup or a jug. Try and imagine one of these items. See it clearly in your mind. Know what it feels like – whether it is rough pottery or smooth porcelain. Is it light and delicate or is it heavy? Is it useful or purely ornamental? Does it have ornate and intricate designs upon it or is it simple and uncluttered? Above all – do you like it?

(b) You have practised using your imagination to visualise a room with which you are familiar at the present time; you have spent some time creating the image of a remembered room from your childhood; now you can have the fun – and it is fun – of creating your ideal room in your imagination.

Begin with the basic dimensions of the room – the height and shape of it. What type of window does it have? Remember, this room is a figment of your imagination, so you can fantasize to your heart's delight. The window can be modern plate glass, a latticed cottage window, or anything else you wish. Now take note of the colours which prevail in your room – visualise the walls, the curtains, the furnishings. As you continue with the process you will become more and more aware of the furniture and the ornaments in your room. And, of course, just as in reality you can change things around in any room in your home, you can alter any part of your imagined room which does not please you – it doesn't even cost you anything!

This room is yours and yours alone. Each time you practise this particular exercise you will become more familiar with it and more comfortable with the image you create.

(c) Having created in your mind an imaginary object and then an imaginary room, it is time to go on to create an imaginary scene. This is an opportunity for you to let your powers of visualisation take you anywhere in the world. You can surround yourself with whatever scenery most appeals to you. The weather can be exactly as you would like it to be. If you feel the need to be among people, they can be part of your chosen image; if you prefer solitude, then you can have it. The choice is yours.

Once you have learned to create a beautiful and pleasurable scene in your imagination – and remember that it does not have to be the same one every time – and once you can experience the peace and contentment to be found there, you can be sure that your visual imagination is in full working order and that it is certainly efficient enough to help you in making those important changes in your life.

You will have noticed, I am sure, that as the exercises proceeded the emphasis was placed more and more strongly upon your feelings and emotions. You were asked to be aware of how a particular situation made you feel and what emotions were conjured up by those images of the past. This is because, although we tend to think of imagination as something which is purely visual, the other senses also play a significant role. As you begin to use visualisation to help you achieve your aims, you will need to imagine what success *feels* like as well as what it *looks* like. If you are overweight, you will need to imagine how it would feel to be slim; if you are taking your driving test for the fourth time, you will need to imagine the exultation you will feel when you pass.

The emotions and the images already in your mind have made you what you are at the present time. But, of course, those emotions and images are not necessarily portrayals of the true situation – they have been put there by people and events from your past. There is the world of difference between failing at something and being a failure – but many people do not differentiate. How many times have you heard someone say: 'I can never manage to stop smoking', 'I always have disastrous relationships', or 'I always make such a fool of myself at interviews'? Yet, with determination and with judicious use of the power of your own mind, you can learn to think of yourself as someone who has perhaps failed in some particular area of life in the past – but someone who is going to succeed next time.

Different people naturally react in different ways to the same situation, as you will see from the following example:

Edward and Ralph each decide to enter a tennis tournament to be held at the local club, of which both are members. Edward looks down the list of names of the sixteen entrants for the tournament and says to himself: 'There is some pretty stiff competition here so I'll have to do my very best. I'd better get in some extra practice.'

Ralph, however, looks at the same list of names and thinks: 'Most of those people are far better players than I am so there is no point in entering; I have no hope at all of winning.' It is only because of Edward's persuasive powers that Ralph decides to remain in the tournament at all.

So you can see how, even at this early stage, there can be a tremendous difference in reactions. Because he has been beaten by some of those other players in the past, Ralph is so convinced that he is a failure that he is ready to give up before he even begins. Edward also knows that some of those other entrants have proved themselves to be stronger players than he – but that does not stop him wanting to improve his performance and do his best. After all, there is no world champion in tennis, or any other sport, who has not been defeated by more experienced players when he was at the start of his career. Equally, there is no world tennis champion who has not served a double fault or lost a match – but a real champion will always come back to win again as long as he is physically able. A real champion will never say 'X managed to beat me on the last occasion; therefore I am a failure; therefore there is no point in my playing against X ever again.' He will think to himself: 'Although X beat me last time, I know that I am capable of winning on this occasion and I intend to do my very best to do so.'

Let us go back to our tennis players. Ralph decides that there is no point in wasting time on extra practice as he *knows* that, as soon as he comes face to face with one of the more expert players, he will be knocked out of the tournament altogether. Because of his negative attitude he is actually defeated in the very first round by someone he has been able to beat easily in the past.

Edward puts in a lot of extra practice and he also spends time visualising himself playing to the very best of his ability. Because of the effort put in, he does very well in the first few rounds of the tournament, even defeating some of those who had previously proved to be much stronger players. He does not necessarily go on to *win* the tournament, because all he can do is to play the very best tennis that he is physically able to play. It may be that there is someone who is a more experienced and better player than him. In just the same way, all the visualisation in the world will not guarantee that you get the job when you go for an interview if you are not the most suitable applicant. It will guarantee that you acquit yourself well at the interview itself and that you do not let yourself down through nervousness or lack of confidence. And, of course, when we are dealing with situations where there is no competition – where no one can be 'better' than you – you can be sure of succeeding in your chosen venture. If you have a driving test or an examination coming up, you can be confident that you will perform to the very best of your ability and that means that, if you have done all the necessary preparatory work beforehand, you will succeed.

So please, for your own sake and your own future, take some time to practise the exercises set out in this chapter. It will take effort – but anything worth having always does require effort. Once you have completed them and can rely on your imagination to do your bidding, you are more than half way towards creating for yourself the life that you would really like to live.

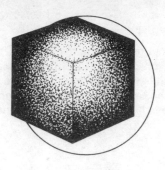

4 · LIGHTS, CAMERA, ACTION!

Having dealt with the theory and worked on the technique of improving your imagination, we now come to deal with the practical aspects of visualisation.

Naturally, as with all methods of self-improvement, there is no one 'correct' way of going about things. What I am going to explain to you are techniques which have been proved to work, but this does not mean that you are not free to adapt any or all of them to suit your own personality. Each of us is different and we must work in our own particular way. What I would suggest, however, is that you *begin* by following the methods set out in this book fairly closely, and only when you feel confident that you have the whole concept of effective visualisation should you vary the techniques in any way your intuition leads you.

The beauty of using the power of your mind to create your own future is that, unlike the making of a film, no million-dollar budgets are necessary. There are no cameras or pieces of sound equipment, no expensive sets to construct, no travelling to find the ideal location or waiting around for perfect weather conditions. Even the writer of the screenplay, the director and the leading actor – all of them you – will give their services freely. Your reward will be the positive changes you will be able to make in many aspects of your own life and the benefits you will feel from doing so.

Not only do you not need special equipment, you do not need to possess any particular powers apart from knowing how to use your imagination (which we have already discussed) and how to relax – which you are about to learn.

RELAXATION

The ability to relax is an essential first step in the technique of visualisation. And relaxation is very different from just sitting down and doing nothing; it is a positive technique – but one which can be learned by anyone. When you relax fully, you are actually slowing down the pattern of your brain waves and allowing yourself to attune with your inner self. You will cease to become aware of your body and be engrossed only in what is happening in your mind. Just as the lights are dimmed in the cinema to enable the audience to concentrate fully on the film, so you will be shutting off the outside world and all its distractions, thereby enabling full attention to be given to the visualisation in which you will be engaged.

Once you have practised relaxation techniques for a considerable time and have become quite expert at it, you will find that you can achieve a state of inner peace anywhere – on an aeroplane, in a train, or in a crowded room. To begin with, however, make things easy for yourself and find a place and time where you will not be disturbed. Perhaps you would feel happiest in your own bedroom, away from the distractions of family life, television, or the telephone. You only need to find twenty minutes or so each day to be able to perfect the technique and, whatever your everyday worries or problems, they are not going to get much worse in the space of twenty minutes, so put them aside and make this your special time.

I am going to give you details of three different methods of achieving relaxation, and it is up to you to find which one suits you best. But do give each technique a fair chance; little will be gained by trying a particular method on one occasion only and then going on to the next. I would suggest that you try each of the three techniques for a week before even attempting to make up your mind which one you prefer. Of course, you may even create your own way of achieving the relaxed state which is a combination of any or all of the methods given here.

You may wish simply to read about the techniques and then put them into practice, or it may be that you will find some assistance useful. There are various things you can do:

1. Record your own voice reading the technique on cassette and then play this as you practise.

2. Ask a caring friend to read the method aloud to you as you practise the technique.

3. Make use of one of the professional pre-recorded relaxation cassettes which are now readily available. (Addresses of distributors are given at the end of this book.)

RELAXATION METHODS

In each of the following cases, it is important that you feel comfortable before you start. Some people prefer to lie down and others to sit upright. If you feel happier lying down, it does not matter whether the surface is firm or soft – whether you choose a bed or the floor – as long as you know that you will be happy to lie in that position for about twenty minutes at a time. If you prefer to sit upright, make sure that the chair you use is comfortable and that it has a high enough back to support your neck and head. Take the telephone off the hook, let everyone know that you do not want to be disturbed – and begin.

METHOD 1

This is not dissimilar to a basic yoga technique, and will probably be very easy to accomplish for anyone who has experience of yoga.

Once you are in your chosen sitting or lying position, close your eyes and rest your hands loosely by your sides or in your lap. Do not cross your feet or ankles as this will cause tension on the nerve endings and you will begin to feel uncomfortable in a very short time.

Tense the muscles in your feet as tightly as you can, almost as though you were trying to fit them into shoes which were two sizes too small. Then let that tension go, all at once, so that your feet feel comfortable and relaxed – you may experience a sensation of warmth or even a tingling 'pins and needles' feeling, but this is quite common and it certainly will not be severe enough to cause you any discomfort.

Now tense the muscles in your legs and your thighs, holding the tension for a few moments before letting those muscles relax.

Pull in the muscles of your body next, being aware of a tightening sensation in your stomach and in your buttocks, before letting all those muscles relax so that your body feels heavy and comfortable.

Next it is time to concentrate on your hands and your arms. Clench your fists and feel the tautness in the muscles of your arms; then let go of the tension and feel your hands and arms become relaxed.

Finally we come to the area of the body which usually carries the greatest amount of tension – your shoulders, neck, head, and jaw. Tighten your shoulders and lift them up towards your ears. Clench your jaw and feel the tension in your head as you frown; then relax and let your shoulders become heavy, your forehead smooth, and your jaw slack; even your eyelids should feel heavy by now.

Now sit or lie in your chosen position, allowing your breathing to become smooth and regular. Spend a few moments listening to the rhythm of your breathing and try to establish a gentle, even pattern before going on to the next part of this exercise.

After some moments you begin to use your imagination. Think once again of your feet and imagine that they are growing heavier and heavier on the ends of your legs, almost as though they were made of lead. Still using your imagination, make that heaviness creep slowly past your ankles, up your legs, past your knees and up your thighs until it reaches your hips. So now your feet, your legs, and your thighs should all be feeling really heavy.

Now do precisely the same thing with your hands. Concentrate on them and imagine that they, too, are growing heavier and heavier, and continue that sensation past your wrists, up your forearms, past your elbows, and up your upper arms as far as your shoulders. By now your arms and your hands should be feeling just as heavy as your legs and your feet.

Next concentrate on the whole of the trunk of your body and imagine this area, too, becoming as heavy as lead. Although, naturally, if there were to be an emergency you would be able to move instantly, try and imagine that to move your body would just be too much of an effort. Let the heavy feeling spread upwards across your chest and your shoulders and then on to the back of your shoulders, the back of your neck, rising finally up and over your head so that even your eyelids and your jaw become really heavy.

Remain in this position for as long as you wish, bringing yourself back to alertness gradually and in your own time.

METHOD 2

Although this method concentrates primarily on establishing a breathing pattern, nonetheless it is essential that you are sitting or lying in a comfortable position before you begin.

Close your eyes and, breathing out through your mouth, place your hands on your ribs so that your fingertips just touch in the centre of your body. Now, breathing in deeply through your nose and then our through your mouth, take deep breaths, making sure that your fingertips part as your ribcage expands when you breathe in and then come together again as you breathe out. Continue in this way for several moments.

Now begin to count silently inside your head as you breathe in and out, thinking 'one' with each intake of breath and 'two' each time you exhale. Gradually let the counting become more important than the concentration upon your hands, which are still placed over your ribs. You will probably find that, as you continue this exercise, your breathing will become shallower and your hands will hardly move at all; this is normal and correct, so do not try to alter it.

Eventually, once the breathing pattern has been established, you will become less aware of the silent counting and the slow, regular breathing will continue almost automatically.

While you are practising this exercise, fleeting thoughts and images may come into your head. Do not bother to analyse these but merely examine them and let them go. This is not a time to make decisions or to question your thoughts; this is a time to relax and to go with the flow of your breathing.

Continue this process for as long as you wish and then, when you are ready to bring the session to an end, begin to breathe deeply once again, becoming aware of the movement of your ribcage and of your hands.

METHOD 3

As with the other two exercises, begin by making sure that you feel comfortable in your chosen position and that you are not likely to be disturbed.

Close your eyes and spend a few moments ensuring that your body is comfortable and your breathing is regular. Now think back to a pleasant scene or event in your life. It does not matter whether what you recall occurred last week or when you were five years old. Begin by remembering the most important aspects of your chosen incident – perhaps you think first of the place where you were, perhaps of your own inner feelings. Take your time while examining all the details of the scene you have selected. Quietly bring to mind as many of the surroundings and circumstances as you can – the weather, the people, the colours, the sounds.

Now take your mind back to the events which immediately preceded your chosen image and those which followed it. Do not try to analyse or question what comes into your mind but merely allow yourself to enjoy it. You do not have to concentrate upon the same image or event each time you practise this exercise – the choice is yours.

When the time allotted for your relaxation exercise has passed, allow the memory gradually to fade and feel yourself becoming more and more aware of your present surroundings – the feeling of your feet on the ground and of the chair or pillow behind your head.

AUTOMATIC VISUALISATION

When you first start to practise visualisation, a great deal of what comes into your mind will be automatic. Unconnected images will enter your head and these may seem to have no relevance to your life or your wishes. Do not be disconcerted by this – it is all part of the learning process and you will be able to control your imagination in time. In the meantime, never try to prevent even the most bizarre of images from entering your mind; merely observe them and then change them in any way you like. After all, you are the director of this production and you can make any alterations you wish.

Because early attempts at positive visualisation often involve only the pictorial image rather than also incorporating feelings and sensations, you may find that you observe the scene rather than feel part of it, rather as you would observe a play or a film as a member of the audience instead of playing a role as an actor. There is nothing wrong in this as a first step – indeed, it is quite common in those who are unused to using their imagination – but what you have to try and do is to become the actor, to put yourself into the scene and take part in it. It may be that, at the outset, you will have to use a mental 'question and answer game' to enable you to do this. Think to yourself, 'What do I see? How does this make me feel?' and so on. As your intelligence supplies the answers, incorporate that sight or that emotion into your visualisation.

Because so much of what you imagine during the early stages of practice may be automatic, do not worry if you do not understand what you are observing. Accept it and, if your intuition tells you that it is likely to be significant, let your mind dwell upon it. If you feel instinctively that it has no particular present relevance to your life, let the thought go on its way, but keep a note of what it was. You would be surprised how many seemingly random thoughts prove to have great significance at a later date, so it is always worth keeping a record of them.

SET YOURSELF FREE

Never believe that you cannot change. An audio cassette, a video cassette and a computer disc have all been programmed and each will have certain information recorded upon it. But each of them, using the proper technique, can have the earlier programming erased when you record over it. In precisely the same way, although you and I have been programmed by the events and people in our past, there is no reason why we cannot 'record over' that previous programming and change ourselves and the way we behave. We do not have to use complicated machinery to do this – merely our own minds. Once you can accept this concept, you are freeing yourself of all those previously accepted boundaries and barriers which have hitherto marred your life.

Take a simple example: one day, when Donald was just a small boy, his mother asked him to carry a dish of sweets from one room to another. Delighted to be entrusted with this way of helping his mother, Donald started to carry out his task but, as he entered the room, he tripped. Sweets went everywhere and the china bowl smashed. His mother – perhaps it was a bad day for her – lost her temper and scolded the little boy for his clumsiness. From then onwards, if ever she gave Donald something to carry or to handle, she would emphasise strongly that he should 'be careful' and 'make sure that you don't drop it this time'. Of course, these admonitions only served to make Donald more and more anxious – he wanted so much to please and to be helpful and he was so frightened of breaking another precious piece of china. Because of his anxiety, he was much more tense – and therefore much more likely to drop the item for which he had now become responsible.

As time went on, everyone began to say 'Oh, don't give anything to Donald to handle; he is so clumsy – he's bound to break it.' Eventually Donald, as he grew older, came to believe these words himself and he developed a fear of touching anything fragile or precious because he saw himself as a clumsy and destructive person. And yet all he had been was a little boy who – like every other child – had once dropped something. The rest was nothing but programming, initially by others and later by himself.

Perhaps this example will enable you to see how, in greater or lesser ways, we are all victims of this programming. However, through positive visualisation, we are all able to reprogramme ourselves and therefore to change the pattern of our lives in the future.

WHAT DO YOU WANT?

Of course, first of all, you must know just what it is that you want for your future – and that is not always as simple as it might seem. What we often grow to think of as our own needs and desires are in many cases things that we think we should want. It could be that we have been convinced by observation of our contemporaries or by the images thrust at us by various elements of the modern media. Or perhaps we are confusing what we want for ourselves with what others want for us. A little further on in this book you will find some charts designed to help you to sort out in your own mind just what it is that you really want for yourself and your future.

Sometimes someone will convince himself that he really would like to have a particular job or profession, whereas all he is doing is attempting to fulfil the dreams or desires of others. (This does not mean that those other people do not want the very best for him, but possibly that they do not really understand him.)

Geoffrey was the only son of a respected doctor. He was a bright boy and did well both academically and in sport. When he was very small he was given a toy doctor's kit, complete with miniature stethoscope, and he would spend hours playing at being a doctor just like his father. Of course, adults found this quite charming in the small child and he was surrounded by such comments as 'I see there's going to be another doctor in the family', or 'You can tell that he's going to be a doctor just like his father.' Eventually even Geoffrey himself was convinced that this was what he wanted to do with his life. His parents, of course, were absolutely delighted and did everything they could to encourage him. Every birthday and Christmas he was given 'appropriate' presents – a microscope or books on biology.

When he reached the age of fifteen, having already chosen the most suitable subjects at school and begun to prepare for his examinations, Geoffrey was hit by a sudden realisation. Much as he respected his father and the work that he did, he himself did not want to enter the medical profession. Poor Geoffrey was really in a quandary. How could he tell his parents that he had changed his mind when they had obviously set their hearts on their son following in his father's footsteps? It would be particularly difficult because he did not know what he did want to do, so he would not have any reasonable alternative to offer them. And so he did nothing – but went on to take his A-levels in the 'correct' subjects before going on to become a medical student.

To everyone's surprise, although he was an intelligent and academic young man who worked hard, Geoffrey failed his final examinations. It was at this point that he came to see me. He had heard about the benefits of positive visualisation and he wanted to learn the technique before he resat the examinations. Although he was able to master each part of the technique individually, Geoffrey told me that he was never able to imagine himself doing well in the examinations or even practising as a doctor. He used the technique perfectly successfully in other situations, but when dealing with a future medical career the 'pictures just would not come'.

What had happened here? Because Geoffrey was, in fact, trying to fulfil someone else's (his parents') dream rather than his own – and because he knew that he was secretly opposed to becoming a doctor – he had been unable to visualise a successful outcome. When he was truly relaxed, Geoffrey was in tune with his subconscious mind and his inner self, and therefore was unable to create images which directly conflicted with desires of that inner self. He eventually allowed himself to rethink the whole situation, decide what it was that he wanted from life and make the appropriate changes. He is now working as a respected art historian, writing and lecturing on his chosen subject.

There are two important points which are raised by this particular case:

1. Although, in one sense, Geoffrey's attempt at visualisation can be said to have failed, in fact it did not. It may not have achieved what was seen as the immediate goal, but it did bring him into touch with his real needs and wishes – it reprogrammed him – and he then had the courage and intelligence to follow this new path.

2. It should not be thought, however, that, just because a particular image is difficult to create or the visualisation is not perfect on the first attempt, you are necessarily looking in the wrong direction. Of course, this is always possible but perseverance is usually necessary in order to achieve success. In other words, if you find it difficult to create a particular image, don't think that you are necessarily trying for something which is in direct contradiction to your subconscious wishes. It could just be that success will take a while to arrive. So give it time and keep practising.

How are you to discover precisely what it is that you do want? Learn to trust your intuition – once developed it is not likely to let you down. And, as you become more adept at real relaxation and the discovery of inner peace, you will also become more aware of what your intuition is telling you. Neil Simon, when being interviewed on American television, said that he always knew when a scene 'felt right'. No matter what anyone else told him – and because of his success there were always those around to flatter him – he relied greatly upon his own intuition. Remember that, like Mr Simon, you are writing the screenplay to this important film and therefore if, at any point, you are not entirely happy with the script, you are the one with the ability to change and rewrite it.

FEEL AS WELL AS SEE

Remember that, for visualisation to work successfully, you need to imagine feelings and emotions as well as pictures. This is yet another way in which you can discover what you really want. If you can imagine a successful outcome to a particular situation and yet are unable to feel pleasure or delight at that outcome, perhaps your inner self is telling you to reconsider and to look closely at your real hopes and desires.

AFFIRMATIONS

Some people like to incorporate affirmations into their visualisation process and, if this is what you wish to do, it can certainly do no harm and may well help you considerably. An affirmation is merely a repeated statement which emphasises verbally your wishes. Many years ago Emil Coué achieved a measure of success with his patients when he would advise daily repetition of such phrases as: 'Every day and in every way I am getting better and better.' Whether it was the actual affirmations or whether it was the patients' belief in their mentor which brought about that success will never be known. I can only say that I have found from personal experience over several years that affirmations alone are not sufficiently powerful to bring about successful outcomes to situations which face you – but, having said that, they can be a worthwhile addition to the visualisation process.

COPING WITH NEGATIVITY

Because of the effectiveness of previous programming, it is not impossible that negative images will force themselves into your visualisations from time to time. There are, however, simple and effective ways of dealing with such occurrences. What you should not do is try to force these negative images out of the picture or pretend that they do not exist. You need to incorporate them and defeat them, thereby ensuring that they have no power.

Natalie came to see me shortly before she was due to take her driving test for the third time. She had been learning to drive for eighteen months and her instructor assured her that she was a careful and competent driver. Indeed, Natalie herself was convinced of this and was quite confident when driving – except when she took a test. Then she would become so nervous and agitated that she was unable to deal with the situation at all.

Having taught Natalie the basic techniques of relaxation and positive visualisation, I asked her to imagine taking her driving test while feeling relaxed and confident. She had to visualise the whole scene, from the moment she first sat in the car with the examiner until the time he told her that she had passed and handed her the piece of paper which confirmed it. For a while everything went well and then, one day about three weeks before her test was due, Natalie came to see me in a very distressed state. After successfully visualising all the events for some time she was suddenly beginning to imagine a situation which would mean that she was bound to fail her test.

She told me that, when she visualised walking with the examiner from the test centre to the car, she saw that two other vehicles had parked immediately in front and behind – her car was wedged in so tightly that she knew she would never even be able to begin her test. Try as she might, she could not force this image from her mind.

I assured Natalie that the last thing she should try to do was to force the negative image out of her mind. What had happened was that, because she had failed her driving test twice in the past, she had come to think of herself as a failure in this sphere. As the date of the test grew nearer the old fears and doubts entered her mind and, since they could not compete with the successful visualisation which was the product of her subconscious desires, the only thing they could do was to ensure that she did not take the test at all. And so the image of the trapped car had come about.

The only way to defeat this sort of negativity is to incorporate it into the visualisation, adding at the same time a method of overcoming the problems which might arise. In Natalie's case I suggested that she imagined getting into the car with the examiner. He would see and understand the situation and because (even though most learner drivers refuse to believe it) most examiners are just as kind and sympathetic as anyone else, he would tell her that, although he would not actually drive her car, he would guide her verbally out of that difficult parking space and that this exercise would not form part of her test. She could then pull into the kerb a little further up the road and it would be from there that her actual test would begin.

Natalie was able to incorporate this into her visualisation and, in fact, only needed to do so on a couple of occasions, for very soon that negative image ceased to enter her mind at all. Three weeks later I received a telephone call from a jubilant young woman telling me that she had just passed her driving test.

POSSIBLE PROBLEMS

There are just a few common problems you may encounter when first you begin to practise positive visualisation, but these are by no means insurmountable. I set them out here so that you can be prepared for them and so that you will not think that perhaps you are doing something wrong if one or more of them should occur. (It does not necessarily follow, however, that any of these difficulties will arise in your case.)

There is always the possibility, particularly for those people who are unaccustomed to experiencing real relaxation, that you will fall asleep during the exercise. This is even more likely if you are practising your exercise towards the end of the day. And yet the end of the day is probably the best time to do so. Indeed, experts claim that the optimum time for visualisation to be effective is either just before you go to sleep at night or just before you wake in the morning. Since it is rather difficult to arrange in advance what you are going to be thinking prior to waking up, the time immediately before sleep would seem to be the most appropriate time for you to practise. If you find, however, that you do fall asleep on one or more occasions, do not let this worry you. For one thing it should reassure you that you have perfected the art of relaxation and, for another, quite often the process will go on in your subconscious mind even though your conscious mind is not concentrating upon it. Even if this does not happen, tomorrow is always another day and anything worth achieving is worth working for.

If you find it difficult to keep your mind from straying off the point and random thoughts persist in intruding, just keep trying. Do not attempt to remove those thoughts by force and do not allow yourself to feel angry or impatient – either of those emotions would be sufficient to dispel any feeling of relaxation you may have achieved and the whole exercise would be wasted for that day. Let the idle thought enter your mind, look at it, tell yourself that you will deal with it later and then bring your mind back to the task in hand. I can promise you that, in the long run, no damage will have been done.

If results do not become evident as quickly as you would like, do keep trying. Some people find that they are able to make desired changes far more quickly than others – there is no right or wrong time for this process to take. In this, as in any other field, persistence always pays off. After all, Frederick Forsyth, author of *The Day of the Jackal*, showed that book to twenty-two publishers before one could be found who thought it was worthy of publication. If he had not been persistent, not only would the world have been deprived of an extremely good book and film – but Freddie Forsyth himself would have been a far poorer man! If he could do it, so can you. Why should you be the one person in the world for whom positive visualisation does not work when it has proved to be so effective for everyone else who has tried it?

Another reason for possible early difficulties may be that you have a subconscious fear of changing. It is actually far easier to stick to what you are used to, and you will have built up over the years a self-image which has been influenced and affected by everyone you have ever known and every circumstance which has ever surrounded you. It could be that the new self-image you are attempting to create is so different from that former one that you are having problems in making the change. But, if your past self-image could be the result of negative programming, there is no reason why your future one should not be the result of programming too – only this time you will be doing the programming yourself.

BELIEVE IN YOURSELF

Above all, believe in yourself and in the fact that you deserve the best out of life. Have faith in your ability to make the necessary changes – albeit one at a time – so that you are able to enjoy your future by becoming the person you would really like to be.

Learning to harness the power of your mind and practising visualisation techniques can never do you any harm at all. If you find that your mind is bringing forward images of the past which you do not like, you have two choices. If you are feeling strong and determined enough to deal with them, you can study these images and learn from them. If you would rather not deal with them at all, you can simply switch off and end the session for that day, beginning again the following day or whenever you feel in the mood. Remember that the choice and complete control are always yours, so the technique can never hurt you; it can only improve your life in whatever way you desire.

STEP BY STEP TO VISUALISATION – SUMMARY

1. Practise using your imagination until you are satisfied that you can not only see images inside your head but can experience the emotions which accompany them.

2. Learn to relax. Practise each of the techniques given until you find the one most suitable for you.

3. Decide what you want out of life and the changes you want to make in yourself. Make sure that you are considering your own wishes and not what you think other people want for you. Use your intuition to guide you.

4. Remember to include all of the senses and your emotions in your visualisation. Affirmations can be useful as an additional form of reinforcement, although they are not sufficient on their own.

5. If negative thoughts or images intrude, look at them and let them go. Do not forfeit relaxation by trying to force them from your mind.

6. Do not fret if you fall asleep while practising – it only goes to show how well you have learned to relax. Try again tomorrow.

7. Be patient; nothing worthwhile is ever achieved overnight. Persevere and, provided you are aiming in the right direction, you are bound to make progress.

8. Never be afraid to change yourself or your life. Even if you are a firm believer in reincarnation, you as an individual will only be on this earth once. You deserve the best and must believe in yourself and know that you have the ability to succeed.

9. Remember that you are always in control of the situation and, should you find painful memories arising which you do not wish to think about, all you have to do is to end that particular session and go back to it the following day.

10. Enjoy yourself. Feel genuine pleasure as you change yourself in whatever way you choose. Look forward to the new you and all that you are going to achieve, whether these achievements seem large or small in the eyes of the world.

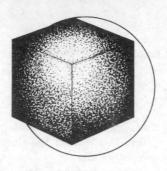

5 · THINK
YOURSELF WELL

With each day that passes, it is becoming more generally accepted that our mental state has a great effect upon our physical health. Naturally that effect can be for better or for worse. It is an acknowledged fact, for instance, that someone who is unhappy or depressed is far more likely to suffer from a cold than someone who is feeling content with life.

Speaking of colds, you will always find some people who proudly proclaim 'I never get a cold' – and indeed they do not. And yet, unless they are living a peculiarly isolated existence, these people must come into contact with the same number of germs and viruses as everyone else. Why then are they not coughing and sneezing or suffering from other typical symptoms of a cold? You have already been given the answer to that question – they *know* that they are not going to have a cold and that knowledge is sufficient to reinforce their immune system and make the belief fact.

The same thing works in reverse. We have all met the individual who says 'I must be run down. If ever there is a cold or flu about, I am always the one to catch it.' And catch it they do. They spend a large part of the winter (and often of the summer too) with blocked noses, rheumy eyes and throbbing heads.

But what exactly does it mean when someone claims to be 'run down'? Simply that their immune system is not functioning effectively – and that is something which can be most effectively corrected by positive visualisation.

I am not attempting to convey here the impression that visualisation makes it possible to do away with doctors, surgeons, and therapists at one fell swoop. Far from it. What it *can* do is work hand-in-hand with other forms of treatment, making them more efficient and allowing the patient to participate in his own recovery. Much of what you will find written in this chapter is effective only when you have consulted the relevant expert to find out precisely what is wrong with you. Of course, self-diagnosis exists, but it is often a dangerous exercise as the patient not only has insufficient knowledge of the workings of his body but, in addition, is frequently in a despondent state which makes it even harder for him to be objective about his symptoms.

The most successful form of treatment – whether by orthodox or complementary medicine – is one which cares for the patient holistically. That is to say, the patient as a whole is treated – as opposed to the symptom. There is no point in giving someone a pill which will disperse a pain in one part of his body if it is merely going to reappear in another.

DEALING WITH PAIN

This is an area where one must be very, very careful. It is quite a simple matter to use the power of your mind to dissolve pain – but it can be a dangerous thing to do. Pain is there for a reason. By getting rid of the pain, you may also be getting rid of the warning which is indicating to you that something is wrong. A headache, for example, may be simply a pain in the head due to stress or tension. But it could also be an indication of trouble with the eyes or even an early warning of the growth of a brain tumour. It is important to know what the problem is.

There are only three situations in which I would suggest that you use visualisation to relieve physical pain:

1. If you know the cause, it is being treated, and your doctor has agreed that you are not likely to do yourself any harm by deliberately removing the pain. If you have sprained your wrist, for example, and removing the pain might cause you to use that wrist before you should, it could be that you would in fact do yourself even more damage. On the other hand, one of my patients, a businessman in his fifties, came to see me because of constant back pain. He had

been to his doctor and had been diagnosed as having permanent fusion of some of his vertebrae. There was nothing which could be done to improve the situation and he did not want to take pills for the rest of his life to alleviate the constant pain. He told me that he could cope quite well during the day but that he found it extremely difficult to sleep at night as the pain kept waking him. This in turn meant that he became more and more tired and therefore found it difficult to concentrate on his work. With the blessing of his doctor, I taught my patient the technique for easing pain which you will find further on in this chapter, and he went on to use it every night when he went to bed, thus ensuring a good night's sleep.

2. If you have been medically checked by a doctor or specialist and have been told that there is no physical cause whatsoever for the pain but that it must be psychosomatic or the symptom of an anxiety state. It is quite safe in such cases to use positive visualisation to remove the pain, although that in itself will do nothing to overcome the emotional problem which caused it to arise in the first place. It would be advisable, therefore, to seek help at the same time to discover and treat the underlying cause of your anxiety.

3. If you know that you have been under a great deal of pressure lately and that the pain you are feeling is likely to be a result of the build-up of tension in your mind which has transmitted itself to your body.

To help you judge whether or not stress is likely to be the cause of your pain, look at the chart which follows. This is a widely accepted list of lifestyle changes which can adversely affect the physical health.

You will see that alongside each lifestyle change indicated in the chart is a score. Look down the list of possible changes and see which, if any, have happened in your life during the last six months. Then total the appropriate scores. Psychologists have proved that if there is a high score for the six-month period (over 300) then there is a strong likelihood of pain or major illness becoming apparent – this will happen to about 80 per cent of the people concerned. If the score is between 150 and 300 points, then about 50 per cent of the people will suffer illness or stress-related pain. If the score is under 150, fewer than 30 per cent are likely to develop pain or illness.

LIFESTYLE CHANGES	SCORE
Death of husband or wife	100
Divorce	73
Marital separation	65
Jail sentence or being institutionalised	63
Death of close member of family	63
Illness or injury	53
Marriage	50
Loss of job	47
Reconciliation with marriage partner	45
Retirement	45
Health problem of close family member	44
Pregnancy	40
Sex problems	39
Addition to family	39
Major change at work	39
Change of financial status	39
Death of friend	37
Change in line of work	36
Change in number of marital arguments	35
Large mortgage taken out	31
Mortgage or loan foreclosed	30
Responsibility change	29
Child leaves home	29
In-law problems	29
Personal achievement realised	28
Wife starts or stops work	26
Starting a new school	26
Leaving school	26
Change in living conditions	25
Change in personal habits	24
Trouble with employer	23
Change in working hours	20
Change in residence	20
Change in recreation	19
Change in church activities	19
Change in social activities	18
Small mortgage taken out	17
Change in sleeping habits	16
Change in number of family get-togethers	15
Major change in eating pattern	15
Holiday	13
Christmas	12
Minor violation of law	11

HOW TO REMOVE PAIN
(once you have established that it is harmless to do so).

A combination of relaxation and visualisation is very effective in the treatment of pain – indeed, quite often you will find that the relaxation itself is sufficient. By its very nature, relaxation reduces the tension in the muscles of the body, so pain is felt less acutely. A natural reaction when pain occurs is to tense the painful area, but this only serves to increase the amount of pain felt. A typical example of this is to be found in women who suffer from menstrual pain and whose natural instinct is to tense the affected area. Quite often, however, if that tension can be eased – either by practising relaxation or even by the application of gentle warmth – the pain will lessen considerably. So if you feel pain, especially if you think that it is stress-induced, practising a relaxation technique three times a day might well be the answer.

There are numerous visualisation techniques which can be used for the relief of pain. Here are just a few, taken from case histories of which I have personal knowledge. But do experiment and find the image which works for you.

1. THE WARM SHOWER

Find a comfortable position in which to sit or lie. Close your eyes and spend a few moments relaxing as best you can. Now picture yourself standing under a warm and gentle shower and imagine that, as the warm water cascades over you and falls to the ground, it is taking with it whatever pain you may have been feeling and washing it away. Spend some time on this exercise and visualise the process in as much detail as possible. Because the warm water will touch your head first, imagine each part of you, from the head downwards, becoming warm and free from pain until finally you come to your feet and your toes. Even after you feel that the pain has washed away, spend some time in your imaginary shower, feeling the beneficial effects of the lovely warm water over your body.

At least one of my patients likes to imagine standing in the sunshine so that her 'warm shower' is actually a shower of sunlight, and it is the rays of the sun which wash over her and free her from tension and from pain.

2. USING INANIMATE OBJECTS

Choose a firm and stable object – perhaps the leg of a table or the back of a chair. Sit by this object and hold on to it, close your eyes and allow your breathing to become slow and even. Then, very slowly, imagine your pain leaving the affected area, travelling down your arm, out through your fingers and into the object you have chosen. Once you feel that you are free from the pain, remain in the same position and imagine a sense of well-being flowing into your body and filling the area which was previously painful.

(Warning – not for the excessively tender-hearted! One of my patients gave up using this method because she said she could not bear to think of all the aching table-legs in her flat!)

3. BREATHE IT AWAY

Relax, eyes closed, in your most comfortable position. Spend some time establishing a slow and regular breathing pattern, counting your breaths silently if you find this helpful. Now, as you inhale, visualise breathing in clean, white air and allowing it to fill your lungs and your whole body. Then, exhaling through your mouth, visualise dark, black, painful air being expelled from your body; you may find it helpful to blow rather than just to breathe out – in this way you are making a more pronounced effort to rid your body of unwanted pain. As always, once the pain has dispersed, continue the visualisation until you are able to imagine that the air being expelled is just as clean and pure as that which you inhale.

4. TAKE OFF YOUR PAIN

This exercise would probably be quite difficult for the beginner but, once you have mastered it, it is very effective. It was used by the gentleman with the fused vertebrae and also a very brave man in hospital who was determined to do without the pain-killers, which caused him such distressing side effects.

Just as you might wear an overcoat on the outside of your body, imagine that your pain is an 'inner overcoat'. Having done the initial relaxation to prepare you, visualise removing that inner coat and throwing it on the floor or, as the gentleman in hospital used to do, hang it on a hook on the wall on the opposite side of the room. He used to say that in this way he could 'keep an eye on it and know where it was'.

TAKING RESPONSIBILITY

Good health is a truly precious gift and one which should not be taken for granted. It is up to each of us to take responsibility for our own health. If we are fortunate enough to be fit and well, it is our duty to ourselves to maintain the status quo. If we are suffering from a particular health problem – or even if at the moment we are just feeling a bit 'run down', then we must play our part in improving the situation. And positive visualisation can help in both respects. But it should not be thought that it is the complete answer. It is a foolish person indeed who claims that he is visualising being well – and then just sits back and waits for the miracle to happen. It may be that medical treatment is necessary – whether it is orthodox or complementary; it may be that efforts should be made to alter the diet, the amount of exercise or the lifestyle of the individual. Relaxation and imagination can play a great part in overcoming health problems, but remember to be sensible and make some positive efforts too.

If you are one of those people who seems to have recurring bouts of poor health, perhaps you should ask yourself some of the following questions:

1. DO I HAVE A HEALTHY LIFESTYLE?

No one is suggesting that you should follow a fanatical regime. There are very few people who are capable of adhering without deviation to a 'sensible' diet, a 'sensible' exercise programme, and a 'sensible' way of life – what boring people we should probably be if we did! But, while a little indulgence will do you no real harm, it is only common sense to ensure that you are getting the right vitamins and minerals, a reasonable amount of sleep, and so on. This is even more the case during periods of less than perfect health, particularly if such periods seem to occur more and more frequently in your life.

2. HAVE I BEEN SUBJECTED TO TOO MUCH STRESS?

Some of the situations which cause us the greatest stress are brought about by ourselves. It is our responsibility whether we allow the traffic jam, the child who will not get up in the morning, or the washing soaked by the rain to cause us to feel tense and pressured. We have far less control over other situations which may occur – the death of a loved one, the increase in the mortgage rate – and these too will bring stress in their wake. But, whereas you may not be able to change the fact that stress has been caused, you *can* diminish the adverse effect it has upon you. A few sessions of relaxation can work wonders for those feelings of tension, the pain in the neck and shoulders, or the stress-induced headaches.

3. HAVE I CONTRIBUTED TO MY OWN DIS-EASE?

Apart from the obvious ways which exist of contributing to your own ill health, there is a certain type of person who is often more likely to attract illness.

Think of the people who always put others before themselves. Now this sounds a worthy enough attitude, but there is often a great deal more behind it. I am not talking here about the normal caring that we show for those we love, or even of those brave people who react so admirably in disasters – plunging into burning buildings, for example, and risking their own lives to save others. The people I am referring to are those who make martyrs and drudges of themselves and whose whole life consists of doing what everyone else wants. On the one hand they choose this way of life for themselves but, on the other, deep feelings of resentment often grow within them. It is also a very strong indication of a particular personality type when someone does not care enough about herself (for this is more often a woman) to think that she has any value at all except as a slave to others.

One of my own patients was a middle-aged woman who could have been quite attractive had she bothered. Her hair was unkempt, although clean, her clothes were practical and sensible and she wore no make-up. She came to see me initially because she was getting one bout of flu after another, although the doctor could find nothing physically wrong with her. Although the family was quite comfortably off, this woman (I'll call her Madge) had no help in the house or with their rather large garden. Her husband would leave the house quite early in the morning and Madge never failed to get up in time to make his breakfast. Then she had to make sandwiches for the children to take to school (these 'children' were in their mid-teens and quite capable of buttering their own bread). From then onward her day seemed to consist of shopping, cleaning, cooking, and pandering to the individual whims of the various members of the family. Son number one liked to have his tea as soon as he got in from school, whereas son number two preferred to do his homework first. Her daughter preferred to eat in her room while listening to music on her cassette-player. And, of course, her husband liked to have a 'civilised' meal without the intrusion of the young people – and, because he liked to relax with a glass of whisky when he got home, he preferred not to eat until nine o'clock. Because of the way in which she had always allowed them to put upon her, not one member of this selfish family gave any thought to Madge until she was ill – and this was happening more and more frequently. (Whether the attention they gave her then was because they were concerned or because their normal pampered routine was being disturbed, I do not know.) Consequently Madge found herself being ill more and more often.

Now these bouts of illness were quite genuine but they were also an indication that Madge's subconscious really wanted her to be pampered and cared for – however often she might protest that she had no time for such nonsense. And it was only after she realised that, although naturally she would continue to look after her husband and children in a reasonable way, she was only harming herself by pandering to their every whim and turning herself into their drudge that Madge was able to establish a routine with which she could cope – and which, after initial protests, her family soon came to terms with. We then worked together to improve her self-image and respect for herself, and the bouts of flu soon became a thing of the past.

There are also those people who have spent their entire lives keeping their emotions in check. Although these people are often extremely sensitive, for some reason – often because of parental influence – they have great difficulty in either attracting or displaying deep emotions. It is only when they are unwell that they can be be treated as the small child in them would like to be treated. Someone will tuck them up in bed with a warm drink; their hot forehead will be soothed and they will be spoken to in loving, caring tones. Being unwell is the only way such individuals have of receiving outward signs of love and affection. Perhaps it is for them that the phrase 'enjoying ill health' was coined.

SEE AND BELIEVE

When using visualisation to help overcome a health problem, it is necessary to do more than see a mental picture of yourself getting well again. You must *believe* that your subconscious mind has the ability to play a vital role in this process. You must *expect* to become healthy once more.

THE HEALING PROCESS

There are several steps to the actual process of healing by visualisation and these apply whatever the particular ailment from which the patient is suffering may be:

1. Relaxation: you have already learned about this vital technique. It is more than simply a preliminary to successful visualisation – it has a definite value of its own.

(a) Relaxation will put you in touch with your subconscious mind, which allows the imagination to fulfil its function without the interference of doubts and questions on a purely intellectual level.

(b) By relaxing your muscles you will actually alleviate pain even before beginning to put your visualisation technique into practice.

(c) Relaxation reduces the element of fear. Think what happens if you are frightened of something. You become tense and rigid, both mentally and physically. By relaxing you are able to dispel that tension which, in its turn, reduces feelings of apprehension or panic. This applies whether we are talking about the natural fears of a cancer sufferer or the more temporary ones of a patient visiting the dentist.

2. Visualise your pain or illness. It does not really matter whether you do this literally or symbolically. There are those who like to be shown an X-ray or a diagram of their precise problem, whereas others will visualise the illness as a dragon or a wolf with long fangs (or some other appropriate image). Whichever you do, it is important that the choice and the image are yours. Do not rely on one given to you by someone else. For one thing it is not as likely to be effective and, for another, it is a way of abdicating responsibility for your own recovery.

3. Visualise any current treatment being effective and successful. Imagine it reducing the actual problem while at the same time reinforcing your immune system. In this way you will be sharing the responsibility for your good health with those experienced professionals in whose care you may be.

4. Having imagined the pain or illness being dispersed, the next stage is to visualise good health pouring into your body, so that you add positive imagery to the dispersal of the negative.

5. Now visualise yourself as being healthy, with no pain, no discomfort, no ill health. Nothing, in fact, to prevent you from

living the full and happy life you would like to live. Remember, when practising this part of the process, to experience the feeling of joy that such well-being brings.

6. Accept that you have played a significant part in your own recovery and give yourself credit for this. Not only is it likely to prevent a recurrence of the initial problem, but you will subconsciously also be taking responsibility for your good health in the future.

Arthur suffered from a painful ulcer which, although not serious enough to require surgery, nonetheless caused him a considerable amount of discomfort despite the fact that he was careful about his diet. He chose to see his problem in the following way: he pictured his ulcer as a room with rough, red, unplastered walls. He imagined his current treatment (the antacids) as plaster, filling in the cracks in these walls and leaving them with a smooth surface. Next he visualised covering those newly plastered walls with clean, pure, white paint; this left the surface cool and smooth to the touch. Then all the debris left by the 'plasterer' and the 'decorator' was swept up and removed. Finally he was able to visualise himself well and untroubled by the normal distressing symptoms which he had been experiencing. He also gave himself credit for having taken the time and trouble to deal with the problem and for playing a part in his own feelings of improved health.

SOME EXAMPLES OF VISUAL IMAGES

If you are to take responsibility for the alleviation of your own health problems, it is you who must select the particular image you wish to use. The samples which follow are methods which have been tried and tested and found to work, but they are by no means the only appropriate images for a particular problem. So try them by all means – but do bear in mind all the time that you are an individual with a mind and imagination of your own and it is up to you to find the image which is most suitable in your own case. (Naturally you should incorporate these images into the complete technique, working through each step indicated above.)

1. HEADACHES (particularly those caused by tension)

With your eyes closed, visualise a piece of pink ice in the very centre of your forehead. As you lie there, imagine the warmth of your skin melting the ice very slowly. As the outer edges of the piece of ice turn to water, see and *feel* that cool, pink liquid covering the whole of the area of your forehead and around your eyes. Not only this, but imagine also the sensation as the coolness from the melting ice penetrates your head, bringing down the temperature on the inside – easing the whole of your head, the area behind your eyes, and the back of your neck.

2. PALPITATIONS, ANXIETY ATTACKS

Imagine that you are looking at a beautiful old grandfather clock. Spend a few moments studying its outer casing, the hands and numerals on the clock face and, finally, the heavy pendulum swinging behind the glass-fronted door. Now concentrate solely on that pendulum, with its slow, ponderous swing. You will find that, as you fix your attention upon that pendulum, your heartbeat and your pulse rate will automatically slow to keep time with it.

3. POOR CIRCULATION

You are walking in a lovely garden, when you come across a small pool. The water in this pool is clear and clean and it has been warmed by the heat of the sun. Take off your shoes and step into this shallow pool. Feel the immediate comfort of the warm water on your feet as the blood begins to circulate freely again, stimulated by the heat of the water. Imagine that feeling of warmth spreading very slowly up your legs so that your lower calves too are warm and relaxed. Now sit on the grass by the edge of the pool and put your hands in the water. Once again the warmth of the water stimulates the flow of blood in your fingertips and then in your palms. Imagine this feeling of warmth spreading slowly past your wrists and up your arms.

4. AFTER-EFFECTS OF STROKE

Mrs Jolly was sixty-two when she suffered her stroke. Although she made a very good recovery and was not affected mentally, even after three years of physiotherapy she was unable to walk without a strong metal frame. This was not too difficult when she was just walking around her bungalow, but it made going more than a few yards down the road uncomfortable, and Mrs Jolly – formerly an extremely independent lady who had lived alone since the death of her husband – found the whole thing most distressing.

Having been told by her physiotherapist that she was unlikely to progress further, and anxious to do what she could to improve the situation, Mrs Jolly decided to learn about positive visualisation. She would imagine herself, first of all, walking unaided across her own sitting-room. Eventually she was able to achieve this. She then went on, stage by stage, to visualise herself walking around her bungalow, down the front path, along to the letter-box and then to the corner shop.

At the end of a period of three months Mrs Jolly was able to walk around her bungalow without any mechanical assistance whatsoever. When she went out she still needed to use a walking-stick – partly to help her manoeuvre steps, kerbs, etc., and partly to give her added confidence – but this was a vast improvement upon the metal frame. Once again she was able to do her own shopping and, even more of a delight to her, to take her rather elderly little dog for short walks.

5. CANCER

It is now widely accepted that not only is a great deal of cancer created by the mind but that much of it can also be reduced or even destroyed by the mind. Whether a patient can be completely cured of cancer depends very much on how far the disease has travelled before the therapy starts. Even in those cases where a cure is not feasible, however, it is often possible to bring about periods of comfortable remission. (For more detailed information about work in the field of cancer, read *Getting Well Again* by O. Carl Simonton and Stephanie Simonton – see Further Reading list).

When working in London, I used to run a cancer self-help clinic which consisted of some of the patients of one particular specialist, and we worked with his knowledge and blessing. The group consisted of nine women ranging in age from nineteen to over seventy. At the end of two years, three of those women sadly had died but, of the remaining six, three had entered prolonged periods of remission where they were able to live and function much more effectively than would have been expected, and the other three actually had no trace of cancer remaining in their bodies – this was borne out by medical X-rays and examinations.

Cancer sufferers often find that they have a need to imagine a 'battle' going on inside them. They need to feel that something has come along which will fight the cancerous cells and defeat them. The images are as many and varied as the patients themselves. Here are just a few of those used by my patients:

(a) The knights on their white chargers (the healthy white blood cells) come along and defeat the fire-breathing dragons (the cancerous cells).

(b) Several cleaning women, down on their hands and knees, scrubbing away at the stain inside the body, using the strongest possible detergents.

(c) The soldiers of the good army killing off the forces of the bad army.

(d) A huge vacuum cleaner sucking up the 'rubbish' in the body.

(e) Pac-man figures destroying the missiles of the enemy (this image was devised and successfully used by a nine-year-old boy with a brain tumour).

It is not being claimed here that visualisation alone is sufficient to overcome cancer – although in some cases it is – but it certainly has a valid part to play in the overall treatment of the disease and can be used hand in hand with any other form of treatment the patient wishes to accept.

WHY VISUALISATION WORKS IN IMPROVING HEALTH

1. It reduces fear and decreases the pain which can hinder recovery.

2. It creates the desire to have a greater degree of recovery than may otherwise have been expected.

3. The mental processes involved influence the body's immune system and the balance of the hormones, so actual physical changes are instigated.

4. It reduces stress.

5. It enables the patient to get in touch with his own subconscious.

6. It eliminates feelings of passivity and allows the patient to feel that he is contributing to his own recovery.

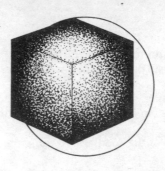

6 • I Think I Can, I Think I Can

In this chapter we are going to discuss the topics of shyness and lack of confidence. These two are strongly interlinked as they are different forms of the same problem. The main difference is that a shy person is someone who is generally timorous and who is likely to feel nervous or awkward most, if not all, of the time. Someone who is lacking in confidence, however, may only be aware of the lack on specific occasions whereas he may be quite sure of himself at other times.

SHYNESS

If one talks about a shy person, it is always assumed that the person being referred to is a woman whereas, of course, the problem can apply just as much to men – often with even more devastating effects. Somehow in the eyes of the world there is something almost appealing about a blushing girl with downcast eyes – think of Lady Diana, as she then was – but the same thing in a man would probably be seen as an indication of weakness.

Shyness always affects people in much the same way. Every sufferer will recognise the physical and mental symptoms shown here – although not everyone will demonstrate all of them on every occasion.

PHYSICAL REACTIONS

1. Blushing: It is interesting to note that blushing only takes place on the face, neck, and throat – where it can be seen by others. This serves to emphasise the fact that it is the shy person's concern with how others see him (or her) which predominates.

2. Perspiration.

3. Acceleration in heartbeat and pulse rate: Quite often the shy person will feel that his heart is beating so loudly that others must hear it and, in extreme cases, the increase in blood pressure which arises causes the temples to throb and the head to be filled with a pounding sound so that he is unable to hear what others are saying to him. At this stage we are really making the transition from shyness to a full anxiety state.

4. Trembling: This can be real or imagined. Even when real, it is not always visible to others (although the shy person will always believe that it is). Trembling knees, for example, are often not noticed by other people, although the shaking hand will be. Sometimes, however, there is just a trembling sensation inside the person themselves of which no one else will be aware. Many actors speak of experiencing this feeling until they are well into their first speech.

MENTAL REACTIONS

1. The mind 'goes blank': A normally intelligent person will suddenly find that, not only can he think of nothing to say to the person in front of him, but he cannot even fully understand the meaning of the words he is hearing. And, of course, the more you worry about this situation, the more your head is full of thoughts of how foolishly you think you are behaving and the worse it becomes.

2. Speaking too much and too quickly: This is really a result of the blank mind syndrome. It is as though the shy person suddenly realises that he has been saying nothing and he feels the need to fill the gap with speech – any speech – as quickly as possible. It is not unusual for people in such cases to say things which are untrue, not because they are liars but because they have to say *something* and so they say the first thing that comes into their head. This sort of situation can also lead to stammering in someone who does not normally have this problem. Indeed, if it arises too often, it can even cause someone to become a constant stammerer.

3. Panic: The need to escape from the situation which is causing the sufferer so much distress can lead to fear of crowds, claustrophobia or even voluntary withdrawal from others altogether.

The situations indicated above are not intended to cause doom and gloom to any shy person. As with anything else, there are degrees of shyness and it does not automatically follow that anyone who is a slight sufferer will ever get any worse. There is one very significant fact which should be appreciated by all shy people, however, and that is that *it is possible to eliminate the problem completely, using nothing but the power of your own mind.*

Those who experience shyness are only shy of people, never of things. And, although that shyness may be slight or it may lead to extreme anxiety states, it is always based on one thing and that is what the sufferer believes other people are thinking about him. It is because the individual is so conscious of how he appears in the eyes of others that he becomes shy and over a period of time he begins to see himself as he thinks others see him.

Shyness itself can lead to all sorts of problems in life:

LONELINESS

Because he is unwilling to make the first approach, it is very difficult for the shy person to make friends. You will normally find that the only friends he will have are those whom he has known for a considerable amount of time. This difficulty is often experienced by women when they move to a new district, particularly if they are at home all day, looking after a young family. They find themselves far away from their relations or anyone with whom they may already have formed a friendship and yet, if they are shy, they are too nervous to make the first move in their new environment in case they are rejected.

BEING PUT UPON BY OTHERS

Although they may often build up inner feelings of resentment, shy people are very bad at standing up for themselves. Because they have been programmed to think that their opinions are valueless – or because they just imagine that other people will hold that view – they are unlikely to express these opinions publicly. It is the shy junior in the office who is asked to stay late and type that urgent report because she is the one who will not have the courage to raise any objection. It is the shy child who misses out when the treats are being handed round because he will not come forward and say 'What about me?'

MAKING A BAD IMPRESSION

There is no point in having wonderful qualifications for a particular job if you are tongue-tied at the interview. There is no point in having a wonderful, caring nature if you are too shy to respond when spoken to by a member of the opposite sex. Inner confidence has nothing to do with outward appearance. It is an aura you carry with you. We all know people who may be neither pretty nor handsome but who attract people to them wherever they go. Such people have an inner confidence – they *know* that they are attractive people. And because they think of themselves as attractive, others do too. This is true charisma and is of far more value than a pretty 'film-star' face with nothing behind it.

NEGATIVE AURA

Because a shy person is one who has no confidence in himself, his whole body language will betray this fact. The way he stands, the way he holds his head, the expression on his face or in his eyes – each of these is saying to the world 'I have no importance and no value.' If this is the aura which is being projected, it is the one which others will subconsciously absorb, so that eventually they come to accept the value you put upon yourself. And so the shy person is trapped in a vicious circle of negativity.

Some people are shy all the time whereas others are only shy in particular circumstances. Many actors and performers are happy to appear in front of a crowd of hundreds – or even thousands – but hate parties of twenty or thirty people. I once attended a dinner party at which the late Peter Sellars was a guest. There were about ten people sitting around the dinner table and for the first half hour or so Peter Sellars did not join in the conversation at all. Eventually he began to speak quietly and in monosyllables and it was only when he started to use some of the multitude of funny voices of which he was capable that he was able to become the 'life and soul' of the party. This great actor had so little confidence in his own persona when in a small

63

group of people that he needed to hide behind artificial characters in order to be able to join in the conversation.

No one is born shy or lacking in confidence. It is something which develops in the child as he or she grows. Of course, if one of your parents was shy there is the possibility that you unconsciously copied what you saw and became shy too. It is not only the shy parent who creates a shy child, however. The adult who is overbearing and dogmatic may have precisely the same effect, as may a brother or sister who is more extrovert or quicker at learning. This programming may be purely on a subconscious level; it does not mean that the dominant adult wanted anything but the best for his child – merely that he did not realise the results of his attitude.

Every time someone says 'I'm shy' they reinforce the condition. The programming is intensified. To overcome shyness – and I promise you that it is possible – requires positive action on your part. It will not go away by itself. There is little point in using tablets or alcohol to hide your shyness as these will merely mask the symptoms and leave you feeling even less confident than before. Alcohol can also make an already nervous person act in a way which is contrary to his nature and say things that he does not mean – so you could end up feeling foolish and embarrassed.

There are three important stages to overcoming shyness:

1. You must believe that it is possible to change.
2. You must want to change.
3. You must work to bring about that change.

If you can accept the first two stages, then positive visualisation will help you to achieve the third. There are no overnight cures, however – no magic wands. Even using visualisation techniques the change will take time. But then, anything which has taken a long time to develop cannot be dispersed in a couple of days. In addition, it is important to start in small ways. There is no point in trying to make the huge leap from being someone who has been shy all his life to becoming the life and soul of the party in one terrific jump.

Two important aspects of your inner beliefs will have to be changed if you are to succeed:

1. How you feel about yourself.
2. How you feel others think about you – and this is often very different from the way they do.

Try this simple test: make a list of what you consider other people think are the good and bad aspects of your personality and character. Try to be as sincere and objective as possible about this – this is neither a time for vanity nor for negativity. Once you have completed your list, ask one or more people whom you can trust to write a similar list (without, of course, seeing yours). When you compare what has been written with what you originally thought, you will probably be quite surprised at the differences.

Sylvia is a young woman of twenty-two with wide dark eyes, long brown hair and a creamy complexion. Younger sister to four strapping, outgoing brothers, she had always considered herself to be the nondescript member of the family. When I first met her she told me that, although she loved her brothers dearly and they in turn were very protective towards her, she always felt timid and insignificant beside them. She had always been quiet and the type of person who found it difficult to be part of a crowd. Even at work – in the busy office of a large insurance company – she felt awkward and uninteresting compared with some of the giggling, chattering girls who worked there. However, when with her permission I asked Sylvia's brothers what they thought of their younger sister, they were full of praise for her gentleness, her serenity and her femininity. At work, too, everyone from her department head to the office junior had a good word to say for her. She was kind, hardworking, and friendly without being 'pushy'. Sylvia herself was astounded to read what others thought of her – but you see how easy it is for someone whose confidence is not strong to see as negative those qualities which others might find attractive.

In some ways shyness can be akin to vanity. After all, the shy person is concerned with what others think about him and believes that he is being watched and criticised all the time. The reality, of course, is that most people are so wrapped up in themselves and their own lives that they tend not be concentrating on you at all. Watch the people walking down any High Street; the majority of them are either looking down at the ground, at the goods in the shop windows, or at the traffic as they wait to cross the road. Even if someone were to be looking at you as they approached, have you ever stopped to think how much time they have to form an opinion of you – critical or otherwise? A few seconds at most. Not even sufficient time to remember what you look like unless your appearance is unusual or eccentric in some way. The same thing applies in restaurants, railway carriages or other public places. Add to this the fact that most people are relatively unobservant anyway – as can be seen from the difficulty they have in giving descriptions to the police when necessary – and you will see how much of your discomfort is a product of your own imaginings.

Someone who is shy thinks of himself as a person with no ability and no value. That opinion has often been put there by others – not always maliciously. The kindest and most loving of parents may well have been so protective towards their child that the same child, when an adult, is convinced that he is not capable of standing on his own two feet. Of course, there are people who try to cover up their own feelings of inferiority by denigrating the characteristics and achievements of others. The husband who repeatedly tells his wife that she is 'stupid'; the parent who insists to a child that he will 'never amount to anything'; the employer who thinks that he can exert authority over his staff by telling them how 'worthless' they are. All these are typical and all too common examples of emotional bullies using unkind words and phrases to hide their own insecurity.

Lisa had been married to Paul for seventeen years when I first met her. Although she had a good job at the time of the marriage, their first child was born after just eighteen months and, because finances permitted, Lisa had chosen to stay at home and care for Susie – and later her younger brother. Paul had a good job but had not risen as far in the company as he had hoped and, for as long as Lisa could remember, he had sapped her self-confidence by telling her that she was stupid and would never be able to obtain or hold down a reasonable job when she decided to return to work. Now Lisa knew that, although not Einstein, she was certainly not stupid, but as she told me, 'When you have been told something every day for about fifteen years, you end up believing it in spite of yourself.' And of course this belief in her own inadequacy led her to give a bad impression at interviews and meant that she did not get a good job. It also gave Paul the chance to say 'I told you so', thereby reducing Lisa's self-confidence even further. It was only when she decided to do something positive about the situation that Lisa was able to put things in perspective and set about changing her inner feelings about herself and developing a positive attitude to life. Because she then had a higher opinion of her own abilities, this was reflected in interviews and she was offered a responsible job at a good salary.

It is only your own ego which can feel embarrassment. Are you frightened of making mistakes and feeling foolish? Why? No one is perfect so you are bound to make some mistakes; so am I; so is everyone else. But it is how we react after making those mistakes which is important. We can apologise; we can try to put matters right; we can acknowledge the errors. And that is all we can do.

Some years ago, when I was first asked to give a lecture on my work, my initial reaction was 'Oh, no. I can't.' But then I stopped to ask myself what I was afraid of. It was not the thought of standing up in front of an audience and speaking – after all, I knew my subject and believed in it. I decided that what I really feared was being asked questions to which I did not know the answer. Once I realised that there is no shame in saying 'I don't know but I will try and find out' the fear disappeared. I was the only one who thought I should be able to answer every possible question and that I would be a failure if I could not. Everyone else would just expect me to be a human being with knowledge about a particular subject – but not a walking encyclopaedia.

Anyone who is shy or lacking in confidence harbours a fear that, whatever they may achieve, those achievements will be unappreciated or even mocked. Whatever you do or whatever you become, you will not please everyone. Have you never looked at a happily married couple and thought 'Whatever did she see in him?' Or perhaps watched a performer on television and wondered how that person could ever have achieved success? Nothing and no one appeals to the whole of the human race. There are many famous artists whose work hangs in galleries and museums all over the world. But would you really think any the less of, say, Turner, because someone happened to admire Rembrandt's work and not his? Whatever you do you will never please everyone – but remember that you are the only person who thinks that you should.

Let us suppose, however, that in spite of having a logical understanding of the situation you are still an extremely shy person with a sense of inferiority and a fear of people and public places. How are you going to use positive visualisation to help you overcome this problem? Try the following exercises.

Remember, first of all, that each exercise should begin with a session of deep relaxation and that you should not proceed to the next exercise until you are confident about the first.

1. Imagine yourself talking to a stranger. There is no need for this to be a lengthy conversation. Perhaps you could ask someone the time. Perhaps you could exchange a few trivial words about the weather with the person behind the counter in a local shop. The important thing is to visualise the situation as you would like it to be; imagine speaking the words while at the same time being calm and relaxed

and the reply being given in the same way. Feel pleased with yourself for dealing with the situation.

Practise the exercise for at least a week before having such a conversation in reality. If you feel that you did well, go on to the next exercise. If you think that you could have done better, try again after another week.

2. Visualise entering a cafe or coffee shop with which you are familiar, ordering some refreshment – perhaps a coffee and cake – and sitting and enjoying it without embarrassment or fear that other people are watching you. If it makes it easier, you could perhaps have with you a magazine to read so that you do not feel so self-conscious.

Once again, this exercise should be practised until you feel able to carry it out in reality.

3. Imagine yourself approaching a person you have met but do not know very well – perhaps a neighbour or someone with whom you work. In your visualisation ask that person to join you for a drink or to come to tea, and see their pleased reaction and their acceptance. Be aware that you are not simply overcoming your own shyness but possibly being of great assistance to someone who may have wanted to get to know you better but felt too timid to make the first move.

As before, wait until you feel quite comfortable with the mental image before attempting to transform the visualisation into reality.

I remember being told a story when I was a child about the little engine who wanted to get to the top of the hill but was informed by all the big, noisy steam engines that he was far too little to succeed. As he went along the track and approached the hill, the little engine said to himself 'I think I can, I think I can.' He kept repeating the words and the thought over and over again until he finally reached the top!

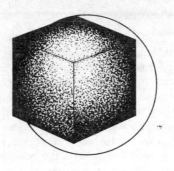

7 · THE POINT OF THE PLOT

However expert a producer, director and cast of actors might be, no filming can take place without a screenplay. That screenplay itself cannot be written unless the writer knows and understands the point of the plot. In this film, in which you are writer, director and leading actor, you have to begin by having a clear understanding of the story and precisely what you wish its final outcome to be. In other words, before you can employ the techniques of positive visualisation you have been learning, you must decide what it is that you want to achieve.

You might think that such a decision would be very simple to make, but it is not as easy as it sounds. There is often a great difference between what we want and what we *think* we want, and this is complicated still further by the fact that we are often greatly influenced by what others want for us. The charts which follow are designed to help you make that distinction and clarify your aims.

Because the type of person you are, as well as your hopes and ambitions, may well change over a period of time as people and events in your life play their parts, it is a good idea to use such charts at regular intervals – say once or twice a year. Keep them all in a file or folder so that you can compare them. Those aims and ambitions which do not change at all will become evident and you will be able to recognise a pattern which should help you in your progress. You will also see in

69

black and white just what you have already achieved, and this should serve to increase your self-confidence and your belief in the value of positive visualisation and the successful application of the power of your mind. There may also be some aspects which once appeared to have a far greater importance than they do after a period of time has elapsed. This does not necessarily mean that you were wrong in what you wrote on the first occasion; merely that you, your personality, and your desires have altered a little with the passage of time.

Before you can even begin to consider your hopes and ambitions, you need to know about yourself as an individual. We are all three different people. We are the people we know ourselves to be; we are the people that others perceive us to be; and we are the people that we *think* others perceive us to be. Try the following test: divide a large sheet of paper into three, with the headings:

How I see myself

How I think others see me

How others say they see me

Complete sections one and two yourself and then ask a few trusted friends or relatives to tell you what to write in section three. You may be surprised at the results – and you will certainly learn quite a lot about yourself.

Now, using the information you have gleaned from a combination of your own insight and the thoughts of other people, complete a chart with the two headings:

What I like about myself   What I dislike about myself

Please don't do it all on one day, as what you write will be affected by how you are feeling. Take about a week to complete it, going back to it each day and seeing whether you still agree with what you have written or whether there is anything you wish to change because it was perhaps coloured by the mood of the moment in which it was written. (Naturally when we are talking about the aspects of yourself that you like or dislike, we are only referring to those about which you can do something. If you are five feet tall and would really like to be six inches taller, that is unfortunate but there is not a great deal you can do about it – except perhaps ask yourself why it worries you). A note to anyone who has thought of many dislikes but no likes – you are not telling the truth!

Study first of all the list on the left, the one which contains those aspects of your personality that you like. If you were to see those comments written about someone whom you had never met, you would think that they applied to quite a nice person, wouldn't you? Why then do you never give yourself credit for those positive traits? Perhaps doing so in the future would give your confidence and your self-image just the boost it has needed.

Now take a look at the list on the right, the one telling you what you do not like about yourself. Look down that list and decide which of those characteristics you would like to change first. List these as below:

Things I would like to change – in order of priority

1.

2.

3.

4.

5.

There are a few generalities which may have found their way on to your list and these will need thought and clarification.

1. If you have said that you would like to be 'more confident', stop and ask yourself just what that means. What is confidence? Confidence to do what? This is far too vague a term and you will need to be more specific. How does that lack of confidence affect you? Does it make you shy in public – or scared of driving – or nervous when taking examinations? Think about it and change that phrase to one which is more precise.

2. If you have written that you would like to be 'happy', stop and consider what would *make* you happy. Perhaps that is what you should be aiming for. Ask yourself why you are not happy now – and whether you should be. In addition, because happiness is such a fleeting sensation, would you be more likely to achieve your aim if you were to substitute the word 'contented'?

3. If you have stated that you would like to have 'the ability to make more money', ask yourself the reason for this. That is not as foolish as it sounds. I know that you would like enough money to live reasonably comfortable and to be able to enjoy the extra pleasures that a good income can bring. But when you wrote of 'more money' how

much more did you mean? If you were thinking about wealth beyond the dreams of avarice – what would you do with it all? Money itself never brought happiness, as the tragedies in the lives of more than one well-known and fabulously wealthy family must prove. There is nothing wrong in wanting money for a purpose, however – perhaps to do some good in the world – but be cautious about wanting riches for themselves.

4. If you have said that you would like to be better organised so that you have more free time, ask yourself – more time for *what*? Finding extra time to spend on a hobby, with your family, or even on yourself, is an excellent idea but it is important when using the charts to carry your ideas through so that you can feel you have a reason for what you wish to achieve.

Here is a little game you can play which has far more to it than you might at first believe:

Remember how in the story the good fairy always arrives to grant three wishes to the newborn baby or the brave hero. Well, I want you to imagine that a good fairy has come to you and told you that she will grant any three wishes *provided* you are able to name them instantly. What would you say? Quickly and spontaneously now – no time to think!

When Daphne, a thirty-eight-year-old divorcee, was asked this question her immediate reaction was to say: I want to be slim, to be married again and to move home. Then she laughed a little self-consciously. 'I suppose I would like to lose some weight,' she said. 'But I haven't really thought about whether I would like to marry again and I believed I was quite happy with my little house.'

If you can play this game honestly you may well surprise yourself at the answers you give when you are not allowed time to think. Even if some of the 'wishes' are beyond your personal control, nonetheless you should gain some very valuable insight into your inner hopes and desires.

In Daphne's case the one thing she could do something about was her weight – and visualisation can help here too. Although the only way to lose weight is to eat less and/or exercise more, visual imagery can be very useful in helping you to attain the size and shape you want. While following your chosen weight-loss regime (and all the sensible ones work if you stick to them), use your imagination at the same time to see yourself in an outfit you would dearly love to wear – but one which only looks good on someone who is slim. It could be something you used to wear but which no longer fits; it could be an outfit you have seen in a shop or magazine; it could even be a product of your own imagination. In fact you can change the mental outfit as often as you wish. The important point is that you have to imagine yourself wearing it and looking perfect. Nothing must wrinkle, stretch or gape. The garment must show off your slim figure to perfection.

There are two main reasons for practising positive visualisation when trying to lose weight. The first is that it is a good ploy psychologically as it keeps that fact of what you are trying to achieve in the forefront of your mind. The second reason is that, although we are limited to a certain extent by our bone structure and our basic shape, by using your imagination in this way you will be able to lose the weight in the areas you wish and your subconscious mind will play its part in helping you to achieve the slim figure which will look perfect in the type of outfit you have created in your mind.

Daphne's second wish – to marry again – was not strictly within her control. She did tell me, however, that over the past two years her life had become rather boring. She worked in a shop during the day and came home each evening to clean the house and prepare the meal for her two teenage children. She was not nervous about going out – indeed, she loved meeting people; it was just that she had got out of the habit of doing so. When asked about it, however, she said that it would not be too difficult to arrange. She was not fanatical about housework, a meal could be prepared in advance, and the children were old enough not to need a babysitter. She could quite easily have a night out with friends or go to an evening class if she so desired. Of course, there was no guarantee that outings of this sort would lead her to meet a future husband – but she certainly wasn't going to find one sitting at home in front of the television.

Although she could not really understand her spontaneous reaction about a change of home, Daphne was quite prepared to put this to one side for the moment. As she explained, taken together with the other two wishes, it showed her quite clearly that what she was looking for was a change in her rather humdrum way of life. Looking at the situation as a whole, she decided that she would make those changes of which she was capable and wait and see what happened with regard to the rest.

When Sidney, one of many junior executives in a large financial concern, was asked to name his three wishes, he said: 'I want a large office with a mahogany desk, a sports car and to be good at golf.'

If we look at those three wishes together, what do they tell us about Sidney? They are all trappings of success in business. A mahogany desk is very expensive and only people in a very senior position can hope to have a large office to themselves. Sports cars are not cheap and, although it is possible to become a good golfer by using the public course at weekends, private lessons and good clubs are also expensive.

When questioned, Sidney agreed that he would dearly love to be a success in the business world but that he felt he had little chance of being noticed in such a vast company. Although he knew that he was good at his job, it did not seem to be worthwhile making any special effort as he felt that he was just one among many.

I asked Sidney whether he thought he had learned anything from playing the wishing game. He said that it had helped to rekindle old ambitions and had reawakened his desire to be a success in business. Although he was not going to give up his position in the large company until he had something better to go to, he had decided to look around for a similar position in a smaller concern – one where he would be more than 'one of the crowd' and where hard work could bring rewards in terms of promotion and appreciation. He told me that his eventual aim was to work for himself – an ambition he had long ago pushed to one side but which he was now determined to reinstate.

So you see how playing this deceptively simple game can help you to gain some valuable insight into your real hopes and desires and, even though visualisation might not always provide the full answer, it can certainly be used in specific areas once you have decided upon a plan of campaign.

USING POSITIVE VISUALISATION TO OVERCOME SPECIFIC PROBLEMS

1. A DIFFICULT RELATIONSHIP

Alison had never really got on very well with her mother. A strong and forceful woman, Mrs Brant had done her best to rule her daughter's life ever since she was a very little girl. This had resulted initially in arguments and tantrums on Alison's part, followed by sullen disobedience until, at the age of seventeen, she just could not stand it any longer and had left home.

After a series of uninteresting jobs, Alison had started work in a solicitor's office and, by attending evening classes and working hard, had eventually progressed to a senior secretarial position. As time went by she married a man ten years her senior and they went on to have twin sons.

Alison's husband was a kind and gentle man and, having never met his mother-in-law, he suggested that they make a journey to visit the older woman with a view to healing the rift between mother and daughter. The meeting was a disaster. As soon as she saw her mother, all Alison's old feelings of resentment welled up inside her and it was all she could do to be civil to her. For her part, the old lady had become more cantankerous and bossy than ever and seemed to delight in finding fault with Alison's appearance, her work – even the way she was bringing up her children. The visit was brought to a speedy end and Alison spent most of the journey home in tears.

It was at this point that Alison came to see me. She felt that something had to be done about the situation. It seemed ridiculous to her that an intelligent adult could still be so wounded by the vicious tongue of a malicious old woman. When we discussed the matter, Alison confessed to me that she also felt extremely guilty. She was surrounded by so much love from her husband and her children and yet she was unable to feel love for her own mother.

Many people have a mistaken idea about filial love. We cannot force ourselves to love anyone – particularly if they act towards us in an unlovable way. The idea that one *has* to love a parent often brings in its wake great feelings of guilt and inadequacy. If parents have brought up their children in what they think is the best way possible – even if that way proves to have been unfortunate – then those children owe their parents respect and duty for what they have done. But no one *owes* a mother or father love; that has to be earned. And just because someone is your mother or father does not make them a lovable person.

Once Alison was able to accept this line of thinking a great deal of pressure was lifted from her. She was even able to feel sorry for her mother who, by her own words and actions, had alienated friends and family and was now a lonely old woman. She felt that it was her duty to take her twins to visit their grandmother but she still did not know that she herself would be able to cope with the situation.

I suggested that Alison arrange a visit for a specific date in the future, giving herself at least three or four weeks in which to practise visualising the occasion. Then I asked her to spend a short time every day visualising the visit taking place and, even though her mother would be unlikely to change the habits of a lifetime and would probably be her usual difficult self, to imagine herself coping and reacting in the way she would like. She would remain polite and unruffled no matter what the old lady said and, on the way home, she would feel really pleased with what she had achieved.

The visit took place about three weeks later. When Mrs Brant realised that all her bitterness was evoking nothing but a polite response from her daughter, just like any bully she ceased attacking. Although there was still no real warmth between mother and daughter, the old lady was genuinely pleased to see her grandchildren and Alison had felt that she had taken a giant step forward.

That was two years ago and Alison still takes her children to visit their grandmother. She will never feel love towards her mother but neither can she be hurt by her any longer, for she can see her for what she is – a rather pathetic woman whose attempts to dominate the lives of all those around her have led her to a lonely old age. For her part, although she cannot undo the foolishness of the past, Mrs Brant is making definite attempts to avoid making the same mistakes with her grandchildren.

2. FEAR OF BEING DRIVEN

When he was in his early twenties Harry was a passenger in a car driven by his older brother. Owing to a mechanical fault the car went out of control as it was going round a bend in the road. It skidded off the road, down a grassy slope and into a clump of trees which fortunately brought it to a halt. Neither Harry nor his brother were seriously hurt, each of them suffering only superficial cuts and bruises, but they were both shaken by the ordeal and were treated for shock by the ambulancemen who were called to the scene. The car, however, was damaged beyond repair.

Once he had recovered from the immediate after-effects of the accident, Harry had continued to travel quite happily in cars, both as driver and as passenger. However, some fifteen years later he had begun feeling more and more nervous when forced to be a passenger in the front seat of a car which was being driven by someone else, although he remained a competent and confident driver. This feeling had nothing to do with the capability of the person driving the car or the speed at which it was being driven. From being a vague apprehension it developed to such an extent that Harry was physically sick at the thought of being a passenger. From time to time he would think of seeking help to overcome this problem – but it seemed simpler just to avoid the situation altogether and to ensure that he was always the one who did the driving. Matters came to a head, however, when Harry broke his arm in two places. Naturally with his arm in plaster he was unable to drive. This meant that his wife would have to take him to and from the office each day in the family car.

Harry came to see me the day after the accident. The doctor had suggested that he did not return to work for two weeks, but he did not know what he was going to do after that. He was not worried about his wife's driving ability; he knew that she was a careful and steady driver, well used to taking their children to school, Brownies, swimming, and all the other places they had to go. There was no way he could get to work by public transport from his home in a small village, but he was beginning to panic at the thought of being driven there.

Harry knew nothing about visualisation but he was prepared to try anything. After teaching him the basic techniques of relaxation, I asked him to imagine sitting in the front passenger seat of the car with his wife in the driving seat and then to picture the scene as his wife drove around the block from their home and back again – a journey of approximately four minutes. All the time he was to be aware of a feeling of peace and relaxation. Once he had done this for a few days, Harry was able to get into the car and allow his wife to drive him around the block and, although he did not particularly enjoy the sensation, nonetheless he was able to remain calm and unflustered.

The next stage involved visualising his wife driving him a mile down the road and back home again – still concentrating on feelings of relaxation. This too was achieved some days later.

Finally, four days before Harry was due to return to work, he was to visualise the entire journey from his home to the office. As before, he was to concentrate on feeling relaxed and at ease, with total confidence in his wife's driving.

By the time he went back to work, Harry was able to be a passenger in the car and so his wife was able to take him to and from work each day until his arm had mended.

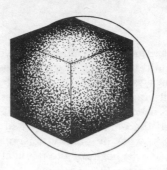

8 · In the Beginning ...

Anything created has first to be imagined. Whether it is the artist standing in front of a blank canvas, the writer contemplating a white sheet of paper, or the sculptor gazing at a huge slab of cold stone, the hard work has to be preceded by imagination. No creative person will just begin working and see what happens. That does not mean to say that he cannot deviate dramatically from his original idea as one part of what he is creating leads to another, but the basic concept is essential in order for him to begin.

We are all born with the ability to be creative. And we are not talking here only about the painters, writers, and sculptors of this world. The businessman with a successful plan can be creative, as can the scientist conducting his experiments, or the inventor with his inventions. But in many cases this creativity is stifled at a very early age. How many times have you heard a child being told 'Don't daydream'? Naturally in this as in any other area it is necessary to strike a happy balance. There is no point in having the idea for a wonderful novel if you have never learned to read and write.

Many people genuinely believe that they are not capable of being creative in any way at all. 'I am no artist', they will say, meaning perhaps that they have never mastered the techniques of colour blending or of perspective. But such aspects as these can be learned. Inner creativity is always there – it just has to be released from its prison.

Creativity is just like any muscle in the human body. The more it is used and exercised, the stronger it will grow. However, the reverse is also true, and if it is not used at all it will wither and grow weak. And it is not difficult to destroy the creative confidence of the very young, thereby condemning the future adult to a life where creativity itself plays little or no part.

Gina was a quiet and sensitive little girl with a clear, sweet singing voice. One day at school, when Gina's class was having a singing lesson, the teacher asked her to sing a short solo. Embarrassed at having to stand in front of the entire class and sing, Gina found that when she tried to sing the higher notes of the song, her voice wavered and she was unable to reach them. With the unkindness that children can muster, her classmates laughed at her – one or two of the more mischievous boys even uttering squeaking noises in malicious imitation. Gina blushed a brilliant scarlet and burst into tears.

From that moment onwards Gina refused ever to sing in class again in case she was mocked once more. Oh, she *looked* as though she was singing – she was far too obedient a little girl to appear to be rebellious – but all she ever did was to silently mouth the various songs.

That story is true. It was told to me by the adult Gina (not her real name of course), who is a friend of mine. No one can know whether she would have grown up to have a real talent for music and singing, but at least she would have had the opportunity to find out had her musical creativity not been stifled by mockery at an early age. For never since that time has she had the courage to sing in public, even among a group of other singers. She managed a wry smile when she told me that her own family did not even realise that she only mouthed the words of the carols at the service they all attended each Christmas.

The creative mind can be expanded and developed at any age. It should not be imagined that, because someone does not have a musical or artistic talent, they are not creative. Some people have the ability to create peace and harmony in their surroundings, while others may knit beautiful jumpers or grow lovely flowers in their gardens. Perhaps the ability to create harmony in the relationships which surround you is one of the greatest talents of all.

What is a creative person? It is someone who is willing to see the whole of life as an adventure, filled to the brim with exciting possibilities. He or she is willing where necessary to set aside old boundaries and to discover a new way of looking at things.

As you learn to stretch your imagination you will stretch the extent of your creative mind. So, just by practising the techniques for improving your visual imagination, you have already set out upon what may prove to be one of the most rewarding journeys of your life. The most forward-looking ideas usually come to us in the form of pictures or images rather than as words, so it is the ability to visualise which it is important to develop and improve.

There are three separate stages to the creative process:

1. The individual feeds his initial thoughts and ideas into his mind.
2. A period of time elapses when, although nothing much may appear to be happening, the mind is working on processing those initial thoughts. This period of time can vary from a few short hours to a matter of days – or even longer.
3. The moment when the answer becomes obvious – the flash of inspiration perhaps. This will normally come as a visual image, although sometimes it will be realistic and sometimes symbolic.

HOW TO HELP YOURSELF

Perhaps the first and most important thing is to acknowledge that, however well concealed it may be, a fount of creativity lies within you. No one is born without it – although in many cases our early lives and the people around us have succeeded in squashing the first outward signs. It may be that you are aware of the direction in which your creative talents lie. If that is so then your task is a little easier than it is for someone who has no idea at all. But you can be sure that everyone, regardless of age, status, or academic training, can learn to develop their basic creativity.

FIND YOUR OWN 'TRIGGER'

Everyone has a time of day or an activity during which their mind is likely to be less occupied with the day-to-day problems of living and coping with business or family responsibilities. It is up to you to find yours, for it is at that time of day, or while performing that activity, that you will be best able to free your mind and allow it to attune with your subconscious.

You do not have to be sitting still to achieve this state of mind. Some people find it beneficial to be engaged in some physical activity – such as digging the garden or ironing the clothes – because at such a time, although their hands and their bodies may be working hard, no real intellectual thought is needed. Indeed, many women find that the time spent rhythmically – if rather monotonously – passing an iron to and fro over clean washing is the ideal time for daydreaming and indulging in delicious flights of fancy. All you have to do is to make use of this 'free' time in order to enhance and direct your inner creativity and therefore your life.

Of course, you may be one of those for whom it is essential to sit still, or even lie down, in order for you to release your mind from the mundane. If that is the case, then just indulge in such stillness for a short period each day. All I am asking you to give is about twenty minutes out of each twenty-four hours – not a huge chunk of your time to donate to the wonderful cause of enhancing your life. Naturally, if you are someone to whom such stillness is essential, do try and find a time of day or night when you are unlikely to be disturbed by young children, ringing telephones, or urgent deadlines.

RELAX

By now, whichever method you employ, relaxation should have become much easier for you. Once you have practised a relaxation technique for some time you should be able to slip into a tranquil gear quite easily without even having to go through all the preliminaries. If you do not have this ability yet, then by all means go through each stage of your preferred technique. Even for the expert, it is beneficial to return to the step-by-step method every now and then to reinforce your acquired expertise.

Why should you relax in order to become creative? As we have already seen, it is only in this state of tranquillity that you are able to come into contact with the deeper recesses of your subconscious mind, and it is from this same subconscious mind that all true inspiration grows. So, although you may be able to state intellectually that you would like to paint pictures or write poetry, you could actually be overlooking or even denying some hidden deep desire to be creative in another area.

BE PATIENT

Inspiration will only arrive in its own time and there is nothing you can do to hasten this arrival. Of course, you may be one of those who find that, after only a few days, you are quite certain of the direction in which you wish to travel. But for most of us the longed-for 'flash of inspiration' only hits us after a prolonged period of practising and waiting – rather like all those actors, singers, and musicians who become 'overnight stars' after many years of hard and grinding – and often poorly rewarded – work.

The author Ruth Rendell, whose work has been so highly acclaimed, said that she had been writing all her life and had in fact had books published for fifteen years before she was 'discovered' and hailed as a bright new talent!

LEARN TO RECOGNISE INSPIRATION

Just because you choose to put yourself in the right frame of mind while painting the garage wall, or lying on the sofa, does not mean that this is necessarily the time when your own particular inspiration will come to you. What you are doing by practising these techniques is putting yourself in the right frame of mind for the germination process to begin. A seed sown in the earth in ideal conditions will still choose its own moment to show its first tender shoots, and there is no guarantee that you will be standing there watching at the time. Similarly, your own moment of inspiration may touch you at a time when you are thinking of something completely different, and this is why you must learn to recognise and acknowledge it.

Use your intuition to help you; it will very rarely let you down. Listen to that small inner voice guiding you along the creative path – possibly in a direction you have never imagined. You may find yourself embarking on a fascinating and fulfilling journey.

WRITE IT DOWN

Creative inspiration is such a transient thing and because, as we have seen, it may well come at an unexpected and even inconvenient time, it is important to capture it before it disappears altogether.

Whether the thought which comes to you is an idea for a splendid new novel or a wonderful new invention – or even the answer to a business problem which has been worrying you – write it down! We all think that we are going to remember these brilliant thoughts, but our minds become so cluttered with all the bric-à-brac of life that, unless we take care to note them, they can be lost for ever. It is not necessary to write your ideas in long and comprehensive detail; a few key words and phrases should be enough to encourage total recall.

An eminent specialist in the field of cancer research was interviewed recently on television. This man has been responsible for some of the most significant steps forward in his field. As he told the interviewer, some of his ideas come to him at the most unexpected times – when shaving, for example, or while bathing his infant son.

For this reason he has developed the habit of leaving pads and pencils all over his house, his office, and his laboratory, so that wherever he may be when a relevant thought strikes him he can make an instant note of it. In fact, as he went on to say, some of these thoughts and ideas do not seem at first glance to take his research any further forward and yet, when he looks back some time later, they have been responsible for guiding his mind in a particular direction.

DO YOUR HOMEWORK

Inspiration is all very well but it will achieve nothing on its own. If you wish to be creative in any way and to make use of those precious ideas, you must first know your subject. You will not write a wonderful concerto if you do not know what each of the instruments in the orchestra is able to do. You will not paint a masterpiece if you have no idea of form or perspective. You will not create a brilliant new recipe if you are not aware of the result of blending various ingredients. Whatever your chosen direction, practical abilities play a large part.

Visualisation is used to help a student overcome examination nerves – but it is only part of the process. If that student does not do any revision in his chosen subject, he will not succeed. Provided he has done his homework, however, positive visualisation can help him to see himself as a success and will therefore prevent him letting himself down through nerves.

If you are about to take your driving test, there is no point in thinking that you can escape having to learn the highway code or how to do a three-point turn. Visualisation will not do that for you. But the majority of failures in driving tests come about because of the state of nervous tension and the lack of confidence of the person taking that test. And in that area visualisation will certainly help you. Provided you have done your homework you can learn to think of yourself as a success and to believe that you can achieve what you set out to do.

DO IT!

Don't waste all that precious hard work. Start the action as soon as you possibly can. It does not matter if the first results of what you set out to achieve fall short of your ideals; anything worth having is worth working for. Many of the most famous chefs began as humble kitchen-boys and the greatest artists as paint-mixers for their masters. The saddest people are those who talk about the books they *could* have written, the garments they *could* have designed, or the pictures they *could* have painted – if only . . . You do not have to be one of those people. You have at your fingertips and in your subconscious mind all the knowledge and intuition you need to become a truly creative person. Oh, you may never be another Picasso, Molière or Einstein – but you will live a more fulfilled and therefore a happier life. And what is the alternative? To wait until you are ninety and then to look back and say 'if only'?

HELP THE CHILDREN

In all but a few special schools, classrooms today are very left-brain oriented. Everything is logic and fact; there seems to be no room for the use of the imagination. This is not to say that logic and fact do not have a vital role to play in the acquisition of knowledge, but imagination and the expansion of the young mind should be allowed to play their part too.

In spite of all this emphasis on the left brain, it is right-brain activity which brings forth creativity. And creativity does not only refer to painting or story-telling; there is no one more successful than the businessman whose creative ideas give him an advantage over all his competitors. Without creative minds there would be no scientific discoveries, no inventions. But only someone whose mind has been allowed to roam free is capable of creative thought and inspiration.

Not only is there far less place in the classroom for the use of imagination – in so many homes the child's leisure time is spent in front of a television or a computer keyboard. The child who spends hour after hour staring at a television screen becomes so mesmerised by the medium that both the excellent programmes and the mindless ones run into each other. And for every child who uses a computer creatively and inventively, there are hundreds who spend their time playing games and following programmes invented by others, allowing them no time at all for free and creative thought.

I always remember the story of the little boy who claimed that he far preferred listening to plays on the radio than watching them on television because the pictures were better!

In the homes of more enlightened families there are still little children who play for hours with imaginary friends and who believe implicitly in the existence of Father Christmas and the tooth fairy. But many other young minds are forced to shut down their creative activity or to think of it as something to be ashamed of by being told not to 'be silly' or to 'stop daydreaming'.

Of course it is easier to sit the young child in front of the television than it is to read to him or to encourage him to read for himself thereby opening a whole new world of imagination. But these children are our creative adults of the future. They will become our scientists, our artists, our inventors – and the teachers of the following generation. Surely they deserve the opportunity to develop their creative imagination at as early an age as possible.

A schoolteacher friend of mine is in charge of a class of nine-and ten-year-old children in a nearby school. He proves daily how well children learn by developing and using their powers of imagination. He was telling his pupils about life in one of the Third World countries of Central Africa. After explaining about the climate, the terrain, the vegetation, etc., he took them through a guided visualisation where the children had to imagine in great detail living in that particular area. They 'saw themselves' looking at the insides and outsides of their homes, taking note of what vegetables they were able to grow in their small plots of land and having the knowledge that they and their families would have, for the most part, to live on what they could grow for themselves. They were encouraged to experience the feeling of the heat of the sun and the dust on the ground. They imagined wearing the native clothes and caring for the animals which were kept in that part of the world. The whole process only took about ten minutes but the picture was so firmly planted in the minds of the young pupils that they will never forget it.

SLEEP ON IT

Let us suppose that you have a problem facing you to which you have to find a solution. It does not matter whether the problem is great or small – here is a technique which will help you to come up with an answer.

1. When you go to bed at night, immediately before you settle down to sleep, take yourself through a basic relaxation programme, concentrating on making your body heavy, your breathing slow and regular and your mind free of tension.

2. Visualise your problem. If you can translate it into images, so much the better. But if your particular problem is one which is more abstract try one of the following:

(a) Imagine the question to which you would like the answer being written on a huge piece of white paper or on a giant screen. See each word appearing, letter by letter, until the whole question is before you.

(b) Visualise yourself asking the question. Remember that imagination incorporates all the senses, so you might actually hear yourself asking the question, one word at a time. You do not even have to visualise the person to whom you are speaking; whether you wish to think of it as a wise man, your inner self, or some spiritual guide does not matter, as long as you are able to believe that the question is being asked of someone who is wise enough to be able to supply you with the answer.

3. Imagine that you have discovered the answer and have achieved the desired result. Remember to experience the feeling of delight that such an outcome would give you.

4. Allow yourself to drift off to sleep. This should be very easy, even for those who normally have difficulty sleeping, because you will be more relaxed than usual. Some people find that, after practising this routine for a day or two, they may fall asleep during the actual process – but this does not matter. Provided you start the ball rolling, your subconscious will take care of the rest even while you sleep. Think of it as putting a pre-recorded cassette into a player and then walking out of the room. The cassette will still play through to the end, even if you are not there to listen to it.

5. When you wake and before getting out of bed, make a note of the first thoughts to enter your mind, however trivial or irrelevant they may appear. (It is a good idea to keep a pad and pencil always beside the bed to register those initial waking thoughts.)

6. Repeat the process every night for as long as necessary. It may be that you will be given your answer after just one night, but it could well take several days. Sometimes this is because your subconscious needs more time in which to process the information, and sometimes it could be because you have difficulty in recognising the answer once it has been revealed to you.

7. Study your early morning notes and see what pattern emerges and what conclusion this enables you to reach.

8. Once you have found the solution to your problem, allow yourself to feel genuine pleasure at what you have been able to achieve by using the power of your own mind.

A FEW FAMOUS THOUGHTS

'The imagination may be compared to Adam's dream – he awoke and found it truth.'

(Keats' letter to Benjamin Bailey, 1817)

'We are such stuff as dreams are made on; and our little life is rounded with a sleep.'

(William Shakespeare, *The Tempest*)

'Was it a vision or a waking dream? Fled is that music – Do I wake or sleep?'

(Keats, 'Ode to a Nightingale')

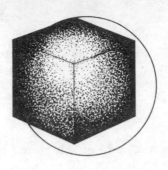

9 · ANYTHING YOU CAN DO, YOU CAN DO BETTER

There is no area in your life in which you could not do better by making use of positive visualisation. Whether you wish to perform better in your favourite sport, to clinch fantastic business deals, to succeed in examinations, to make impressive speeches and presentations – or just to live a more fulfilled and more satisfactory life – imagery and visualisation can help you achieve your goals.

THE WORLD OF SPORT

It is not only the prospective Olympic athlete who wishes to improve his sporting prowess. This desire applies to anyone who has ever felt, or wished to feel, the exhilaration which accompanies the knowledge that you are performing your chosen sport to the very best of your physical ability. It has long been accepted in both the United States and the Soviet Union that outstanding performances are the result of both physical and psychological training. Indeed, in both those countries each national team has not only a coach for the physical aspect of the sport but also a permanent psychologist whose task it is to help the athletes and team members to prepare themselves mentally and emotionally for peak performances.

What this psychological training, always incorporating visualisation techniques, achieves is to allow each person to perform to the very best of his or her ability. It is not intended in any way as a substitute for physical training, but it can certainly enhance and dramatically improve the results which can be obtained from physical training alone.

As part of his research the hypnotherapist and psychologist Romark worked with several different football teams during the 1970s. He was involved in fifty-two different football matches, working always with the team which was considered the 'underdog'. In each of those fifty-two matches the team which had been taught visualisation techniques was the winner – there were not even any drawn games.

In team sports it is often possible to ensure a victory for the team whose members have practised visualisation. If you think about it, in any team consisting of several people it is likely that more than one will be feeling a little off colour. Perhaps one has a touch of toothache; another may have had a disagreement with a wife or husband; yet another may be anxious about his tax returns. If you can ensure that each member of the team, because of the visualisation technique that he has been practising, is able to clear his mind for the duration of the game of all but the desire to win and the knowledge that he can do so, you can be practically certain of victory, even if the team of which he is a member is not believed to be as strong as their opponents.

When it comes to individual sportsmen and women, however, use of visualisation does not necessarily cause the individual to win – but it will make him perform better than he has ever done before. After all, it is possible for two runners competing in the same race to practise visualisation techniques, yet only one competitor can win – and that is the one who is physically more able than the other. You will also find, however, that the other runner has probably given his best performance ever in that same race.

PSYCHOLOGICAL BARRIERS

In all areas of life – and particularly in the world of sport – we are faced with seemingly insurmountable psychological barriers. It was always claimed that it was not possible for any human being to run the mile in under four minutes – until Roger Bannister did it! After that it was but a short time before the feat was again accomplished.

The barrier no longer existed and so others were able to perform this hitherto 'impossible' feat.

In the same way, it was a firmly held belief that no human being could lift five hundreds pounds in weight. In fact the man who finally succeeded in doing so only managed it because he *thought* he was lifting a lower weight. He did not impose the psychological barrier on himself. That feat, too, has since been matched by others.

Are you imposing such barriers on your performance? Do you believe that you can only run a certain length of course, jump a certain height or throw a javelin a certain distance? There is nothing to stop you exceeding what you have always thought of as your capabilities. No one can guarantee that you will be the champion of any contest – that will depend upon your physical ability and the amount of time you are prepared to give to training. But you will do far better than you have ever done before and, once you have broken your own barrier, you can progress from strength to strength.

POSITIVE AFFIRMATIONS

Many famous sports personalities use a combination of physical training, visualisation, and positive affirmations to help them reach optimum fitness prior to an event. You only have to think of Mohammed Ali and his 'I am the greatest' statements. Of course, Ali was a great showman and loved all the attention, but there was also a far more serious side to all those declarations of just how he was going annihilate his opponent. Every time he made one of his positive affirmations, he was in fact reinforcing his own beliefs – 'psyching himself up' – in order to convince himself of the validity of what he was saying. Of course, what he was doing at the same time was undermining the self-confidence of many an opponent – a fact of which he was quite well aware.

AUTOGENICS

Autogenics was developed from forms of hypnosis and self-hypnosis. It was found that some people were resistant to the suggestions being made to them under hypnosis yet would react very favourably to the suggestions put there by their own minds. The first steps of autogenics are not dissimilar to those of the relaxation techniques you have already seen, except that this process relies on six specific stages:

1. *The right arm* (if right-handed; the left arm for left-handed people): imagine the right arm becoming heavier and heavier. If necessary visualise it as being encased in a heavy plaster cast or attached to a lead weight.

2. *The right hand* (or left hand for a left-handed person): imagine that this hand is growing warmer. The more you concentrate, the warmer it seems to become. You may even be aware of a tingling sensation which is a little like pins and needles but which will not hurt.

3. *The pulse:* imagine the beat of the pulse being steady and strong. If you like, try to 'hear' the rhythm of your pulse inside your head. As you concentrate on the pulse, your heartbeat becomes stronger and more regular.

4. *The breathing;* concentrate on establishing a slow, even rhythm of breathing. Do not worry too much about whether you are breathing deeply or not; it is that slow, regular rhythm which is important.

5. *The solar plexus* (the area immediately above the navel): imagine this area growing warmer and warmer. You may find it easier to do this if you picture the heat in the form of bright light entering and filling this part of your body.

6. *The forehead:* be aware that your forehead is cool and relaxed, although not too cold. Because your head is cool and is not tense, your mind too will be cool and in control.

As you will see, autogenics does not merely concentrate on relaxation and feelings of heaviness, but also on warmth in your body and coolness in your head. It is important to follow each step in the correct order and to spend as long on each stage as is necessary in order to feel the appropriate sensation. It is not enough merely to repeat statements to yourself such as 'My hand is warm' – you must actually persevere until you really can *feel* that warmth before progressing to the next step. Although the technique may take you quite a long time at first, you will find that with practice you are able to become aware of the required sensations quite rapidly.

The real value of autogenic training, particularly in the field of sport, is that it enables you to prepare mentally and psychologically. In fact, even if you stopped there and did not progress to the visualisation stage, you would find that you were in a better physical condition and an enhanced state of readiness to give of your best.

VISUALISATION

Having increased your general sense of well-being through auto-genics, you then need to utilise positive visualisation to help you achieve your aims. There are various methods, some of which are indicated here – but remember that you are the director of this film and you can change any scene in whatever way you wish. Indeed, the more the screenplay is adapted to suit you and your personality, the better the resulting performance will be.

EXTERNAL CONDITIONS

One technique which works particularly well with such people as competitors in track events and participants in winter sports is visualisation of the conditions which they are likely to face when taking part in their chosen sport. A runner, for example, is encouraged first of all to get to know a track in reality – either by walking or jogging around it or, if this is not possible, by studying film sequences which show it and talking to others who have run it before him. In this way he will become familiar with the special features of this particular track, learning which parts of it are likely to cause him problems, having regard to his individual style and technique. Once he is confident that he knows the track really well, his visualisation should incorporate all the possible pitfalls which might arise and how he will overcome them. When he comes to perform on the track itself, he will not be taken by surprise by any of its characteristics but will already have programmed himself to overcome them.

PERSONAL PERFORMANCE

There are two separate aspects to visualisation with regard to personal performance. The first is to improve results in general terms and the second is to deal with any specific problems which may arise from time to time.

1. Improving results

The following technique has been found to be extremely satisfactory – provided, of course, that you have continued to train in the normal way.

Marcia was a keen tennis player. She played at her local club and was keen to do well in their championships, although she had no aspirations to take the game any further – no thoughts of playing on a national or international level crossed her mind; she just wanted to enjoy her tennis and play as well as possible.

Although quite a skilled player, Marcia's tennis was somewhat erratic as she often allowed her temperament to get in the way of her performance. If she began to feel that she was playing badly she would become annoyed with herself, and that very annoyance would cause her game to deteriorate even further. In many matches Marcia was not defeated by her opponent but by herself. Once she 'lost her cool' she would begin serving double faults or driving the ball straight into the net.

The initial part of Marcia's training through visualisation did not involve an opponent at all. She was encouraged to take things one stage at a time and in each instance to spend several days on visualisation before attempting to practise what she had been imagining. Her programme went as follows:

(a) Standing at the baseline of the court, holding her racquet in one hand and a tennis ball in the other. Taking the time to imagine just what those two items felt like – the weight of the racquet, the texture of the ball. Then throwing the ball into the air and serving to the opposite court, but not attempting to be particularly brilliant or to serve unreturnable aces. All she had to do was to imagine that every ball she served landed in the correct part of the court; none went into the net and she never served a single double fault. While seeing this scene in her imagination she had to know that on each occasion the ball would land just where she wanted it to and that her feet would remain firmly behind the baseline.

(b) Once she had practised the first stage actually on the tennis court, Marcia was asked to imagine serving with an improved technique. She visualised hitting the ball harder so that it travelled faster and landed precisely where she wanted it to land. Once again, it was not just the pictorial image which was required but also the effort involved and the exhilaration experienced.

(c) The next stage involved the cooperation of a tennis-playing friend or coach. Marcia visualised being able to return every ball which came towards her over the net – and to return it so that it was still within the boundary lines of the court. She was not concerned at this point with placing the ball so that her opponent could not reach it but simply with the ability to return each one, using both backhand and forehand. When she came to practise this exercise in reality, her friend was asked not to try to score points but to send balls over the net so that Marcia would be able to reach and return them.

(d) Having practised returning every ball which was sent to her, Marcia was then asked to visualise being able to make more difficult returns – to imagine having to run all over the court for balls which were out of her reach, as well as coping with those which had been spun or smashed by her opponent. She continued with this particular visualisation for a fortnight before attempting anything more than a gentle game on the actual court.

Although she would never spend enough time on her tennis to become a Wimbledon champion, Marcia found that using this technique enabled her to improve both her confidence and her game beyond measure. She was able to win games against players who had formerly been considered to be far superior to her and even to put up a pretty good show when playing against someone with more technical ability than she had. But – and this delighted her even more – she was no longer betrayed by her own temperament but was able to remain cool, calm, and confident in all situations.

2. Overcoming problems

Mike is a professional golfer playing in national and international tournaments. About two years ago he went through a phase when his performance began to dwindle. He still had no problem in striking the ball so that it reached the green, but his putting was letting him down. And, of course, the more anxious he became about his failure to putt the ball satisfactorily, the worse the situation became. Instead of being able to remain calm and in control when standing on the green, he would think to himself 'I mustn't miss this time', thereby reinforcing images of the possibility of failure.

Now I am not a golfer – I have never done more than play on a seaside putting green – but by teaching Mike how to use positive visualisation it was possible to help him overcome his self-perpetuated difficulty.

(a) Mike learned and then practised relaxation and autogenic techniques.

(b) Next he had to imagine that he was standing on the green with the ball at his feet, just a couple of yards from the hole – certainly at a distance which, before he began to have problems, would have given him no cause for concern. He then visualised himself tapping that ball with sufficient strength and accuracy for it to roll straight into the hole. This process was repeated, time and time again, with the ball lying in different positions on the green. (Over the period when he was working with this visualisation, I asked Mike to refrain as much as possible from practising his putting in reality.)

(c) The next stage was for Mike to spend some time practising on the green but in a non-competitive situation. Because he had repeatedly rehearsed his putting in his mind with success on every occasion, he was able to repeat this process in fact when he stood on the green itself. He did not have to learn how to hold the appropriate club or what stance to take – he had known all that for years. It was not his physical ability which had begun to let him down but his mental attitude and, once he had used visualisation to construct the correct state of mind and rebuild his lost self-confidence, all the old skill and technique reappeared. And, of course, once he was convinced that he could successfully putt every ball when he was not involved in a tournament, it was just one small step further for Mike, being a professional already, to do just as well when playing in competitive games.

IMAGINARY ASSISTANCE

Some sportsmen and women have found that being able to visualise some imaginary form of assistance has actually helped them to improve their performance dramatically.

Jay is a marathon runner living in the Los Angeles area of the United States. He has his own particular visualisation to help him overcome the fatigue which strikes so many long-distance runners. He has been using positive visualisation to improve his performance for many years, but it was only about eighteen months ago that he added a new dimension to this technique.

While practising his visualisation, Jay imagines a large hand beside him all the time he is running. In his own mind he knows that that hand is there to give him help and support – a 'helping hand' in every sense of the word. When he reaches a point where exhaustion threatens to take hold, Jay simply imagines himself holding onto or leaning against that hand, which in turn provides the 'prop' or the impetus that he needs until he regains his own strength. This visual image becomes so real to him that it remains with him during the course of an actual marathon so that, whether he needs to use it or not, it is there to help him. He told me that in many instances the knowledge that he has this imaginary hand to lean on is enough to ensure that he does not in fact need to do so.

Sally is shooter for a ladies' netball team in the south of England. Naturally she spends a great deal of time in physical practice; she also has been using visualisation for some considerable time and has found that it has improved her performance beyond measure. One of the images she uses is that of magnets attached to both the goal net and to the netball itself. This magnet ensures that the ball will be irresistibly drawn to the net from wherever Sally may be standing when she takes her shot.

Of course, such imagery alone will not make a proficient goal shooter. Sally had already learned what physical movements were involved in throwing a ball so that it would land in the net. The visualisation gave her the added concentration and confidence needed to make her one of the most sought-after and successful team members.

Those two examples indicate how two different people used visualisation to create extra help for themselves in their chosen field. If you feel that this particular type of image will help you, it is up to you to select your own visual aid. Do not be afraid of making it ridiculous or larger than life; quite often the slightly outrageous picture – such as Jay's huge disembodied hand – is the one which is easiest to imagine.

HERO-WORSHIPPING

Most people involved in either individual or team sports have their idols – the people in their own field whose sporting prowess they most admire. It often helps in visualisation if they can imagine themselves playing exactly like their hero or heroine. One footballer in Yorkshire even went to the lengths of substituting a photograph of his own head for that of his idol on a team poster. In addition, when he watched television programmes or videos of the player he admired so much, he would imagine himself as that person, performing the feats he was performing. When he came to play in actual matches, our Yorkshireman was able to think of himself as his hero and was able to play far better than before.

THE WORLD OF BUSINESS

Positive visualisation can make all the difference to the life of the businessman or woman. There are so many ways it can be used to harness thoughts, improve relationships with others and reduce stress. Given below are four different business situations and how to deal with them using visualisation techniques, but there is no reason why you cannot extend the range of areas where benefit might be felt.

1. ORGANISATION OF TIME

A tremendous amount of time is wasted in all organisations, large and small, because of lack of planning. The efficiency of the individual – and therefore of the company – is drastically reduced. Reduced efficiency also leads to reduced profits, so you can see that we are dealing with a very real problem.

It does not really matter whether we are talking about the typist who has a desk piled high with reports to type and letters to answer or the company director who has to arrange meetings, delegate tasks, and concentrate on long-term future plans – the problems can be dealt with in precisely the same way.

(a) Sit down and make a list of all your current tasks, however trivial they may seem.

(b) Read through your list several times so that you are familiar with everything on it.

(c) Now, close your eyes and relax, using your preferred method. Imagine that you are sitting at a desk with three large boxes in front of you. One is labelled 'urgent', one 'more important', and one bears the sign 'less important'. Also in front of you is a pile of sheets of paper and on each sheet of paper is written one of the tasks from your list. Visualise picking up the pieces of paper, one at a time, studying *and understanding* what is written on it and then placing it in one of the boxes. Continue until you have come to the end of the pile of papers.

(d) When you have ended your period of visualisation you will find that you have priorities far more clearly identified in your mind. All that remains is to act according to those priorities. In this way you will find that your desk is cleared far more quickly and you do not cause yourself unnecessary aggravation by wasting time trying to decide what to do next.

2. COPING WITH PROBLEMS

This is a way of helping you to deal with whatever difficult situations arise in the course of your business life – and naturally these will vary from one person to another. Whether you have to deal with members of the public, with the interruption of constant telephone calls, with the mistakes of subordinates – or simply with the VAT man – there is much to be gained by remaining calm throughout the situation, as:

(a) The situation will be dealt with far more quickly, thus allowing you to get on with whatever other tasks may lie before you.

(b) If you remain calm and controlled, it is far more likely that the other person will too. You will therefore find them easier to deal with, and more amicable results are likely to be reached.

(c) You will avoid the effects of stress caused by being unable to cope with the problems which arise in the life of everyone involved in business. Apart from the fact that stress makes you far less efficient, it also damages your health and makes you more prone to a vast variety of illnesses.

Select the problem area in your business life (if there are several, choose just one to start with – you can go on to deal with the others later). Having practised your chosen relaxation technique, visualise yourself dealing with the situation in a calm and controlled manner. Concentrate while you are practising on your breathing, ensuring that it is slow and regular. Imagine that you are coping with the problems and annoyances in just the way you would like and that, because of your attitude, the attitude of any other people concerned is also calm and relaxed – no raised voices, no angry gestures. You may have to practise this routine over a period of time before it begins to have a marked effect on your daily life but, provided you persevere, you can be sure that it will.

3. MAKING DECISIONS

Whether you work for yourself, are employed by someone else, or are responsible for the management of a multinational corporation, business life is full of decisions. The more important the decision and the more far-reaching its results, the harder it will be to make. And sometimes it is possible to spend so much time thinking about and around the matter that it becomes more and more difficult to come to any conclusion at all – let alone be sure that the conclusion is the correct one. This is yet another case where visualisation can be of assistance.

Martin had been running his own business since being made redundant from a large organisation some six years earlier. The business had built up gradually, although it was still essentially a one-man show consisting only of Martin, one assistant, and a part-time secretary/bookkeeper. Although he was not making a fortune, Martin was quite happy with the progress he had made. Then, quite unexpectedly, an opportunity presented itself which might enable him to vastly increase his turnover, but to do so he would have also to increase the size of his company by employing more staff and finding larger premises. Another factor to take into account was that there was no guarantee that, once this particular job had been carried out, others of similar size and reward would follow. Martin was in a quandary, being faced with several choices:

(a) He could enlarge his company and take the chance that other equally remunerative jobs would be available.

(b) He could try to expand gradually – which would mean turning down the present opportunity.

(c) He could continue just as he had done for the past few years – this would bring him sufficient money to live quite comfortably and pay his bills, but no more.

Martin thought about this decision for a while, talking it over with his wife and listening to the 'expert' advice of friends and colleagues, but all that happened was that he became even more confused and uncertain of which path to follow. Eventually he was advised to use visualisation as an aid to making up his mind. On each of the following three nights when he went to bed, he would follow a relaxation pattern and then select one of his possible choices, following through in his mind all the consequences of making that particular choice – from the immediate results to the long-term effects. By the end of those three nights he found that he was able to come to a clear decision.

Although this example concerns a businessman, the same method is just as effective when any vital decision in your life has to be made. By seeing things clearly at a time when your mind is quiet and uncluttered – and by seeing the various choices one at a time instead of trying to compare several at once – your subconscious will help you to sort out the tangled web your conscious mind may have created. In some cases all that is needed is the visualisation itself and the answer will then become obvious. In other cases, where the direction to take is perhaps less clear, the accumulated experience and knowledge of the subconscious mind is needed to supplement logical thought.

4. DEALING WITH PEOPLE

No matter whether you are employer, employee, or customer, there are always times when dealing with others can be difficult. The employer may find that he has to hire or fire one of his staff, to reprimand someone, or to ask them to take on an extra workload. The employee may wish to ask for more money, make a complaint about unfair treatment by another member of staff, or even make a suggestion which might improve the efficiency of the workplace. A customer may need to make a complaint about unsatisfactory goods or service – and, even when customers *know* that they are in the right, they will often feel diffident or embarrassed about stating their case.

This situation arises in all aspects of life, not just in the world of business. There are always times when you know that something has to be said but you are not quite sure how to say it. Perhaps you do not wish to hurt or embarrass the person to whom you need to speak; perhaps you do not wish to arouse aggression on their part; or perhaps you have always been rather timid and are not sure how to put your point of view. In each case the technique is the same:

(a) Calmly and logically, sit and work out what would be the ideal approach to make, even if you feel at this point that you would not actually be capable of making it. If you are already familiar with the personality of the individual to whom you have to speak, how do you think he or she will react to what you say?

(b) Having decided in the conscious part of your mind what would be the ideal approach, it is time to use your subconscious to help you. Use your chosen method of relaxation and then visualise the situation exactly as you would like it to take place. You already have your script; now you must direct the cast – and that means you! In your mind see yourself saying the words in just the right way, allowing yourself to be calm yet determined to make your point. Follow this by visualising the reaction you hope the other person will show. Repeat this 'rehearsal' several times in your imagination before shooting the final 'take' and you are sure to find that your performance is vastly improved.

Even if the particular problem area of your life does not appear in the examples in this chapter, I am sure that by now you will see how the process works and will be able to adapt it satisfactorily to suit yourself. Remember that it is the combination of talents of the director and the actor which produce a perfect performance – and since both of them are you, you just cannot go wrong!

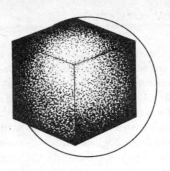

10 · REMEMBER, REMEMBER . . .

How many times have you complained about your poor memory – either that it never has been very good or that it is deteriorating as you grow older? It was at one time thought that memory inevitably grew worse with advancing years, but this is not in fact so. There are, of course, certain illnesses which involve the destruction of a large number of brain cells bringing in their wake a certain amount of confusion and memory loss. But, unless you have the misfortune to suffer from such an illness, there is no reason at all why your memory should be any worse when you are seventy than it was when you were twenty.

Can you remember your address, your date of birth, and the names of your children? You can? I thought you would. If you can remember those things there is nothing at all wrong with your memory. Ask yourself why you remember those particular things and you will realise that they are all important to you. We all hear so much and have so many pieces of information thrust at us during the course of our lives that our mental filing system tends to put anything which seems unimportant or irrelevant in the dusty old boxes in the back of the attic, whereas other things which are more likely to be needed are kept near at hand.

It is not really memory which is in need of improvement, therefore, but observation, concentration, and recall. Our ability to recall stored pieces of information improves with use. This is why it is often easier to bring to mind the telephone number of a friend than it is to remember your own. After all, you are far more likely to dial someone else's number. However, if you are one of those people who states the number each time you answer the telephone, you will have no difficulty at all in recalling it – you use it so often.

Take the example of a young man invited to a party at the home of a friend. On entering the room, he finds that, apart from the person who invited him, he knows no one at all. Every person there is a stranger to him. Suppose that the friend takes this young man from group to group, introducing him to all the people in the room. It is unlikely that our young guest will be able to recall more than a few of the names of those whom he has met – even minutes after meeting them. But now let us suppose that during the course of the evening he is introduced to a young woman whom he finds extremely attractive – he will be certain to remember her name. Why? Because, whatever the outcome of the initial meeting, at the moment of introduction the name of that particular young woman becomes important to him.

Quite apart from the fact that it is useful for each of us to be able to rely on our ability to recall names, dates, and pieces of information, there are certain situations where this ability is essential. Students studying for examinations, businessmen and women who need to know the names of contacts, those who have to make presentations or give speeches – to all of these people total recall is vital. And all of them, with a little practice, can use visualisation techniques to improve their recall to such a degree that it need never let them down again.

STUDYING FOR EXAMINATIONS

The very word 'exam' is likely to instil fear and dread into the hearts of many. And these emotions alone are sufficient to make learning and absorbing what you read difficult, if not almost impossible. There are several ways in which visualisation can help, both with the learning and recall process and also with maintaining calm and reducing panic while actually taking the examination itself.

People vary tremendously in the way they respond to different learning processes, and it is essential to find out what sort of person you are. Do you find it easier to absorb information that you read or are you more responsive to the spoken word? Perhaps you need pictorial images to accompany the facts. Try different methods of learning and see which suits you best.

1. THE WRITTEN WORD

Even those who enjoy reading and who find that this is the best way for them to absorb information lose a certain amount of this ability when faced with a situation involving pressure – such as a pending test or examination. It is quite possible to read several pages of a textbook, not skipping a single word, and to find at the end of it that you have not taken in any of the meaning of what you have been reading. The first stage, therefore, if you know that it is essential for you to absorb information from what you are about to read, is to approach the whole subject in a state of relaxation. So, before even opening the book, practise whichever relaxation technique you prefer; I can assure you that the ten minutes or so spent doing this will save you far more time in the long run by doing away with the necessity to re-read page after page.

Most textbooks contain vital facts hidden among a multitude of words whose only purpose is to make those facts into neat sentences and paragraphs. You must learn to separate the key facts from a plethora of words. Imagine for a moment a page from a history book. Because the author is trying to tell a story, he is doing more than just listing salient pieces of information. You will often find, therefore, that on a complete page of text there will be no more than half a dozen points which you have to know in order to be able to reproduce that story in an essay or in answer to a question on an exam paper. Perhaps there will be a couple of names, a date, and two or three actual events. Underline these facts or, if you do not wish to mark the book, simply make a list of them on a sheet of paper. Now close your eyes and relax and visualise those facts being written by a piece of chalk on a giant blackboard inside your head. Let the words appear letter by letter until the name or phrase is clearly written.

Repeat the process after each page or at each natural break in what you are reading. It is best to stop when you have no more than about six key facts to visualise. At the end of the period of revision, repeat all the facts which you have already seen written on that imaginary blackboard during the course of the session.

2. THE SPOKEN WORD

You may discover that you are one of those people who finds it difficult to absorb information by just reading the material placed in front of you, but that you respond more readily to hearing the spoken word. If this is the case then, instead of listing those key facts which are so important to your studies, you could record them on a cassette. Then, having first relaxed, play this cassette to yourself, making sure that you actually *listen* to the words which are being spoken and that you understand what is being said.

3. THE PICTORIAL IMAGE

Perhaps you find pictures easier to absorb and to remember than words, whether written or spoken. If this is so, then you need to translate the key facts you have selected into images in your mind.

Suppose we go back to that history book. Perhaps you have to read and absorb information about Christopher Columbus. First of all, close your eyes and imagine what he looked like. It does not matter at all whether the picture in your mind is anything like the real Christopher Columbus; the only important thing is that you conjure up a picture of a man who is *to you* Columbus. You can even make the picture a little ridiculous by allowing him to wear a giant medallion around his neck bearing the initials 'C.C.' In fact, the more amusing the picture, the easier it will be to remember.

Now, don't just learn the fact that there were three main ships which sailed together. Close your eyes and *see* them. Once again, unless you are to be called upon to describe them, it does not matter whether or not the design of those ships is historically accurate; what will matter is that you see the names carved or painted on them – the *Pinta*, the *Niña* and the *Santa Maria*.

Thanks to a rhyming couplet often quoted by pupils and teachers in school, many people already know that:

> *In fourteen hundred and ninety two*
> *Columbus sailed the ocean blue.*

Suppose, however, that you have never heard this little rhyme and yet you still need to remember the fact. Once again, allow the pictorial reminder to be somewhat fantastic. Perhaps one of the ships has a huge calendar hanging from its mast; perhaps Columbus has a wrist-watch which tells the date (it's all right – I *know* he couldn't have had a wrist-watch, with or without date, but we're allowing our pictures to be ridiculous, if you remember). Using this method you are unlikely to forget any of the relevant facts, either during or after the examination.

EXAMINATION NERVES

More people fail examinations because of nervousness than through any lack of knowledge – yet this is something you can prepare for well in advance. Use your ability to visualise and imagine yourself in the exam room, feeling calm and relaxed. See yourself turn over the paper and pause for a moment before reading the questions slowly and calmly and then picking up your pen and starting to write. Practise this visualisation for at least three or four weeks before the date of the exam itself and your mind will associate the test situation with feelings of calm and control.

REMEMBERING NAMES

There are many occasions when you may be introduced to someone and told their name but, because you know that you are unlikely to meet that person ever again, the name does not stick in your memory. Sometimes, however, it is much more important to recall names and even more essential to connect them with the right faces. This is particularly true in many business situations where future sales, contacts, and profits may depend upon the impression you make upon the person you meet. Since most people have quite a high estimation of their own importance, that impression is not likely to be a favourable one if you forget their name.

Remembering names becomes far easier if you allow your sense of the ridiculous to come to the fore. As you are given a name, conjure up an image to go with it – the sillier the better. Here are just a few examples, but I am sure that you can think of many more for yourself:

Marian – whatever the age and status of the lady concerned, imagine her in a wedding gown with a huge bouquet. (Marian = 'Marrying' – see?).

Henry – don't tell the poor man that you see his head balanced on the body and legs of a hen (or even laying an egg!).

Rosemary – imagine the lady being cradled in the heart of giant rose.

Adrian – (this one had me foxed for a while when I was first in a situation where I had to remember it). A man in warrior's outfit striding along the top of his wall (Hadrian, of course).

To become accustomed to this technique, you might even spend a few pleasant moments creating images to go with the names of your friends and family – but perhaps it would be better not to tell them what you are doing, particularly if some of the images are *really* ridiculous!

That is all very well, you might say, but what about surnames? Surely these are far more difficult to deal with. Not at all. Many surnames are already words (such as Steel or Brown), but let us deal with a few examples here of those which are not:

Garwood – the person is sitting in a car made of wood, held together with huge nails.

Hatfield – the man or woman dancing around in a field wearing a very large and somewhat outrageous hat.

Daniels – see him in a cage face to face with a ferocious-looking lion.

Hemmingway – a long street lined with people, all looking exactly like the person whose name you have to remember, each of them stitching the hem of a skirt.

And so on . . .

MAKING SPEECHES

Suppose you have to make a speech or a presentation and you do not wish merely to read from a written script. How are you going to be sure that you remember all the things you want to say?

First of all, we will assume that you have some knowledge of your topic – or no one would have asked you to speak in the first place. Now, even if you do not want to read your speech, it is useful to write it in full. This will give you some idea of how long you can allow for each issue and will help you to get your ideas in order. Having written it, go through it in the same way that the student must go through the pages of his textbook and list the points you wish to make.

It is necessary for you now to learn that list of points, and there are several ways of doing this. You can use any of the methods given earlier in the section on studying, or you can use the peg system (of which more at the end of this chapter).

Once you are completely familiar with your list, use a combination of relaxation and visualisation to imagine yourself making that presentation or giving that talk in front of an audience. At the same time, although you do not need to imagine yourself saying every single word, make sure that you deal with each point on your list one at a time. By combining this image with a relaxation technique your subconscious mind will associate giving the talk, remembering the list, and being calm and at ease. Your confidence will grow each time you practise and, when it comes to giving the talk itself, you will be able to remember the points you wish to make and to elaborate upon them without those feelings of panic which so often accompany speaking in public.

THE PEG SYSTEM

Everyone at some time has to remember a list of items. Usually these items are linked in some way – what you should put in your suitcase when you go on holiday, the ingredients of a cake, or which bulbs you wish to plant in your garden. But there is a simple method of recalling lists which works even for unrelated items. Once you have read the explanation you might like to experiment and see just how simple it is.

1. YOUR PEG WORDS

I am going to assume for the purpose of this exercise that your list will consist of ten items. However, the system is exactly the same for any number of objects, as you will see. The first thing you have to do is to list the numbers one to ten and then, beside each number, write a simple noun which rhymes with it. This system will be even more effective if you use the first noun which comes into your mind. The list below will show you the words I use – but it is up to you to choose your own.

```
One   – bun
Two   – shoe
Three – tree
Four  – door
Five  – hive
Six   – sticks
Seven – Heaven
Eight – gate
Nine  – line
Ten   – hen
```

Those words never change. No matter how many lists I have to remember, my peg words remain the same. This is why it is so important that you choose your own words; if you try to use those which do not come naturally to you, you will merely make the system more complicated.

2. THE LIST

I asked five people to name two objects each, completely at random and spontaneously. These are the ten objects which make up my list:

a table
a duck
an umbrella
a clock
an elephant
a television set
a Christmas pudding
a window
a house
a raspberry jelly

3. THE LINK

The next stage is to link each item to one of my peg words. The object is to make the visual image as ridiculous as possible. Thus item one is a table. One = bun. Now to put a bun on a table is not particularly ridiculous – but to use a table on top of a bun instead of a cherry . . .

Continue in this way until the list is complete. These are the images I selected – maybe you would have chosen something different:

One (bun) – a table
A sticky bun with a table on top in place of a cherry.

Two (shoe) – a duck
A duck using a shoe as a rowing boat, holding the oar in its beak.

Three (tree) – an umbrella
A fruit tree which has umbrellas growing on it instead of apples or pears.

Four (door) – a clock
A door which is in fact a huge rectangular clock face.

Five (hive) – an elephant
A swarm of yellow and black striped elephants trying to force their way into the tiny entrance of a beehive.

Six (sticks) – a television set
A television set, complete with aerial, balancing precariously on a large pile of sticks.

Seven (Heaven) – a Christmas pudding
A flaming Christmas pudding with large white wings, flying up to Heaven.

Eight (gate) – a window
A room in a house where every window looks like a glazed five-bar gate.

Nine (line) – a house
A sheet of paper with a margin ruled down the left-hand side – but this margin is made up of dozens of tiny drawings of houses.

Ten (hen) – a raspberry jelly
A fat and contented hen looking rather pleased with itself having just laid an egg made of raspberry jelly.

4. THE RECALL.

Provided you are able to visualise the ten images in the first place, you will find that you will easily be able to recall them either in sequence or in random order. All you have to say to yourself is 'one – bun' and you will immediately see the bun with a table instead of a cherry. If someone gives you the number 'eight' for example, because you are so familiar with your own peg words, you will see a gate and then a room where all the windows are gates – so the word is window.

Remember that, for this system to be effective, it is absolutely essential that you create your own peg words and your own images. I have given you mine as examples only. Go on – try it.

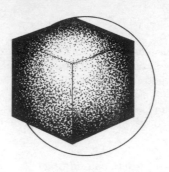

11 · BELIEVE IT OR NOT

Until now we have been looking at the many and various ways in which you can use positive visualisation to improve aspects of yourself and your own behaviour. Up to this point you have been the star of all those films you have written and directed. But what about that other genre – the documentary films in which you yourself do not feature (or if you do it is only in an indirect way)? Believe it or not, the power of your mind and your imagination can work magic here too.

It is a fact that, by using positive visualisation, you can have many of the things that you would really like. This is no new idea but one which has been in existence for centuries. The Ancient Greeks believed it; in fact, if a woman became pregnant they would surround her with items of beauty – statues, carvings, ornaments, etc. – so that all she would see during her waking hours would be beautiful things. This, they thought, would lead her to think of beautiful things when she was asleep, and her subconscious therefore would be so filled with beauty and perfection that the child she produced was bound to be perfect too.

There are three essentials when it comes to using the power of your mind to obtain what you want:

1. You must visualise the desired object regularly.
2. You must believe that what you imagine will happen.

3. You must visualise the end result and not just the means of obtaining it. In other words, if there is a specific item that you would like to have, imagine that item being in your possession rather than someone handing it to you or even being given sufficient money to buy it.

THE WHITE CARPET

Miriam lived alone in a flat in north-west London. She had been widowed some ten years earlier and her daughter had just gone away to study at the University of Southampton. Having worked in an office all her adult life, Miriam had reached a stage where, although she was not likely to starve, there certainly was not an abundance of money. She had recently decorated her entire flat and what she really wanted to provide the finishing touch was a white carpet. Not just any old white carpet, but one of those with a luxurious thick, deep pile. In fact she had always wanted a white carpet but had never felt it to be a practical proposition while her daughter was still at home. However, the carpet she wanted far exceeded the money available to spend on a floor covering.

Miriam was already a firm believer in the power of positive visualisation, having employed it many times during her life. Now she decided to see if she could use it to get the carpet she so desired.

Every night when she went to bed Miriam would close her eyes and imagine that every room in her little flat was fitted with a beautiful, thick, luxurious white carpet. She never questioned the method by which it would arrive. She certainly did not visualise having sufficient money to buy the carpet – her common sense told her that, even if the money should miraculously appear, she would find something else to spend it on and would not be able to justify spending it all on something as extravagant as a pure white carpet.

One day when Miriam was in the office, her immediate superior, who had just married for the second time, announced that she and her new husband were moving to a large house in the suburbs. Almost in passing she mentioned that the whole ground floor of the house was covered with a pure white carpet and that, with four children in the family, this would have to go. Miriam could not believe her ears and, when she mentioned her own longing for a white carpet, her companion said that, provided she could take it up and remove it, Miriam could have the carpet for a nominal sum.

Having quickly accepted the offer, Miriam enlisted the help of her brother and together they took up the expanse of white carpet and, having cut it to fit, they re-laid it in Miriam's flat. Her dream was fulfilled; she was overjoyed with the appearance of her flat; her visualisation had succeeded.

PARKING THE CAR

No matter where you live, parking the car is becoming more and more difficult but, with the aid of visualisation, you can be sure to find a space just where you need it. I know that this sounds somewhat far-fetched but try it for yourself and you will see.

If you know that the area you wish to park in is heavily congested and that parking spaces are normally few and far between, it is best to start the process prior to leaving home. As you sit in your car, before you even turn on the engine, close your eyes for a few moments and visualise a space big enough for you to park in and situated just where you want it. Naturally, there is no point in trying to imagine the impossible – no yellow lines will miraculously disappear just to accommodate your vehicle. But, if you imagine a space where you would like it to be – and provided you believe in what you visualise – when you turn the corner, there it will be, just waiting for you.

This method can even work when you forget to do it before you set out on your journey. I was once due to visit a friend who lived in a street in which it was always difficult to park. Normally I would visualise 'my' space before leaving home but on this occasion my mind was so full of other things that I forgot. I was just turning into the road where my friend has her house when I realised that there was not a single parking space to be had. I was annoyed with myself for forgetting and, almost without thinking, I actually said out loud 'Hey, where's my parking space?' As I said it, a car pulled out into the road from a position right in front of my friend's house, leaving just enough space for me to park my own car.

HOUSE FOR SALE

When Trevor and Elaine first bought their house they had expected to stay in it for several years. Two years later, however, Trevor's job took him to another part of the country, some two hundred miles away. This naturally made a move of home essential.

The property market was going through one of those periods when selling was very difficult. Even though their house was pleasant and well cared for, it was only one among many which were for sale in the same part of town. The estate agent's board duly went up in the front garden – but nothing happened.

Trying to sell a house is always a stressful business but in this case it was made so much worse because, until it was sold, Trevor and Elaine were forced to spend most of their time apart. Trevor's new job had already started and they could not afford to buy another house until the present one was sold, so Elaine had to remain in the existing house while her husband lived in bed and breakfast accommodation during the week, returning home only at weekends. Elaine was becoming more and more depressed. Then someone told her about visualisation.

Each night when she went to bed, Elaine would lie there and imagine the estate agent's board in the front garden. She would see the name of the company and then, in huge letters, the word 'SOLD'. She did not try to work out who would buy it or why they would choose their house instead of one of the others on the market. She just visualised the 'sold' notice – and believed that it would happen quickly.

Just four days later a young couple came to see Elaine and Trevor's house and decided that it was just what they wanted. They made a reasonable offer, which was immediately accepted!

CLEARING THE ROAD

Have you ever been stuck on a winding road behind a swaying caravan or a slow-moving farm vehicle? Of course you have. So what do you do? All the frustrated expletives in the world cannot make those vehicles move any faster and might not do your blood pressure much good either.

Next time you find yourself in this situation, concentrate hard on visualising that vehicle turning off the road or pulling into a roadside petrol station or cafe. (Don't close your eyes when doing this one or you will find yourself in a lot of trouble!) If you have confidence that it will happen, you will soon find your road is clear again as the dawdling vehicle removes itself from your path.

I have been using this method successfully for years – so I would like to take this opportunity to apologise to all those drivers of caravans or farm vehicles who have suddenly found themselves taking an alternative route or having a hitherto unwanted cup of tea!

SEE FOR YOURSELF

I am sure that many of you reading this chapter will be thinking that it is just not possible to influence events in the way I have described. All I can tell you is that each example mentioned here is genuine (apart from the names) and that many people – including myself – have sufficient personal experience to believe implicitly in the power of the human mind when used in this way.

There is only one way to prove whether something works or not and that is to try it for yourself. Try using visualisation techniques to influence events in your life, but remember that you have to have absolute faith that you will succeed. It is also as well to remember that this technique should never be used to harm anyone else (in spite of my somewhat flippant remarks about sending caravan drivers all over the country) or you will find that it rebounds on you in some unexpected way.

So, go ahead and try. You may even come up with some new ways of using that most powerful of tools – your imagination.

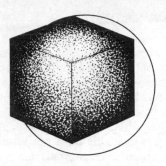

12 • SUMMARY

1. Make up your mind that you are going to take control of your life and your future as far as is humanly possible. You are going to write the screenplay, direct the film, and play the lead.

2. Remember that no one is born without confidence. We have all been 'programmed' by people and events in our lives and, just as it is possible to reprogramme a cassette or video tape, you can reprogramme yourself for the future.

3. Exercise your imagination. Be sure to include other senses apart from just the visual. Imagine hearing, touching, tasting, and feeling the complete range of emotions. Learn to use both left and right brain.

4. Let your dreams work for you. Develop a technique for remembering them; keep a note of them; try to understand them. Practise feeding a problem into your subconscious just before going to sleep so that you can be guided in the right direction when you wake.

5. It is absolutely essential that you learn a relaxation technique. Practise those detailed in this book for at least a week each so that you can best decide which is the most suitable for you. It is possible that you may decide to adapt one of the techniques in some way so that it is more appropriate for your personality.

6. Decide what it is that you want to do or to become. Be as specific as possible. It is better to tackle several problems one at a time than to try and visualise yourself as a 'perfect' person all in one go. Listen to your subconscious.

7. Learn to cope with any negativity which might arise and to deal with any possible problems. If you find the process difficult at first – keep trying. Anything worth achieving is worth working for.

8. Believe in yourself and in the power of your mind and your imagination. Never be afraid to change.

9. Use visualisation to help overcome health problems and to maintain a sense of well-being. This does not mean that other forms of treatment, whether orthodox or alternative, are not necessary. Whatever treatment you may decide to have, its efficacy can be enhanced by the use of positive visualisation.

10. Use charts to keep an on-going record of how you see yourself, how you think others see you, and how other people say that they see you. Note the changes and improvements as you use visualisation to change your life. In the same way, from time to time list the things about yourself that you like and those that you do not. Which of these things would you most like to change? Practise making three wishes!

11. Use visualisation to improve relationships, to overcome phobias, to improve your sporting prowess, and to develop your creativity – whatever form it may take.

12. If you have or work with children, encourage them to develop and use their imaginative powers. Although naturally they have to study their lessons and do their homework, never criticise them for 'daydreaming', as it is in this way that the imagination is set free.

13. Practise autogenics to enhance your sense of inner health. This is particularly important for those who are keen to do well in some area of sport, but it is also helpful for anyone who just wants to develop an inner sense of well-being.

14. Positive visualisation can be of great assistance in the world of business. Use it to organise your time more efficiently, to cope with problems as they arise, to make decisions, and to improve your relationship with the people who work for you.

15. Whether you are studying for examinations, making speeches and presentations, or simply wish to improve your everyday memory, visualisation can be of great assistance provided you are willing to practise the methods suggested. You can remember the names of those you meet as well as lists of objects, whether related or not.

16. Use the power of your mind to affect situations around you – find those parking spaces, sell that house, etc.

17. Start now! Why wait? Set the scene, learn the script, put on your greasepaint – action!

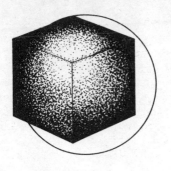

FURTHER READING AND INFORMATION

All in the Mind by Dr Brian Roet (Optima, 1987).

Creative Living for Today by Maxwell Maltz (Pocket Books, 1967).

Getting Well Again by Carl and Stephanie Simonton (Bantam, 1978).

Hypnothink by Ursula Markham (Thorsons, 1985).

The Shape of Minds to Come by John Taylor (Michael Joseph, 1971).

RELAXATION CASSETTES

Available from:

The Hypnothink Foundation, PO Box 154, Cheltenham, Glos. GL53 9EG.

INDEX